"...*poetic passion and*

WITH NEW EYES

unflinching honesty..."

"Margaret Becker has been blessed with a passionate voice—not just as a singer, but as a powerful communicator. When she writes, whether it's a song or the prose in this wonderful book, she's not afraid to be vulnerable. She's perfectly willing to share her heart, and in doing so, she helps us illuminate the corners of our own lives and makes us richer for the experience. This book is a treasure readers will cherish for years to come."

Deborah Evans Price
Associate Editor Country/Christian Music
Billboard magazine

"At a time when every Christian musician seems poised to write a book, *With New Eyes* is a revelation. Becker recounts her adventures in faith with poetic passion and unflinching honesty. Yet in offering an intimate glimpse into her soul's unfolding, she also holds up a mirror: Believers will recognize themselves in her stories, and true to the title, walk away seeing things differently."

Lou Carlozo
Chicago Tribune

"Margaret's prose welcomes us into her life with clarity and kindness, and in the company of her words we find a woman at home with herself, her yearnings and fears, and even her frailty. Becker possesses a self-knowledge and confidence that cannot come from anything as passing as beauty or as superficial as fame. Rather, hers is the self-assurance that comes only in knowing that she is loved—absolutely and beyond reason. In short, these essays and entries are glimpses into the place of grace. I can think of no better place to be."

Dwight Ozard
Director of Public Affairs
Habitat for Humanity

"If you're already a fan of Margaret's musical artistry, you will cherish this window she gives you into her soul and the places from whence she draws inspiration, creativity, and perspective. If you don't know her music, you will be compelled to discover how the author of these pages sounds as an artist. And you will not be disappointed."

Frank Breeden
President
Gospel Music Association

"*With New Eyes* show us that God is telling us our story, if we could only see Him . . . Margaret's gift is to reveal the divine in the everyday, to show us Jesus in next-door neighbors and family and even strangers. I was genuinely moved. I felt ushered into a living, breathing faith. Read it and see your own life in new ways."

Reed Arvin
Record Producer and Author

"In *With New Eyes*, singer/songwriter Margaret Becker breaks the binds of a three-minute pop song to put into vivid imagery the life I—and many others, I suspect—long to live, a journey undertaken with an attentive eye to the small moments of grace that interrupt our turmoil, apathy, and confusion. . . . This talented woman has captured her own experiences with an amazing profundity that translates easily to anyone who wrestles with faith, love, loneliness, purpose, and identity."

April Hefner
Managing Editor
CCM magazine

"This astonishing little book provides the reader with equal parts information and inspiration. Yet it is more. . . . I felt as if I had spent an evening with Margaret, listening to her rich, well-crafted stories, drawn in by her intensity and her childlike purity of heart. Most compelling was the realization that *With New Eyes* had not been a 'one-way' conversation. Maggie's tales of God at work in her life allow each one of us to claim God at work in our own. Indeed, her story is our story."

The Reverend Kempton D. Baldridge
University Vicar and Associate
St. Thomas's Episcopal Church

"Margaret Becker has long been a 'must see' and a 'must hear' with her concerts and records. Now, *With New Eyes* makes her a 'must read.' All her music fans will treasure this book, but it will be a treasured blessing for even those who have never heard her great music. I heartily recommend it to all those who know Margaret Becker and to all those who should. That's everyone."

Bob Briner
Author, *The Management Methods of Jesus*

With New Eyes

Fresh Vision for the Soul

MARGARET BECKER

Photography by Ben Pearson

HARVEST HOUSE
PUBLISHERS
EUGENE, OREGON 97402

With New Eyes

Library of Congress Cataloging-in-Publication Data

Becker, Margaret. 1959-
        With new eyes / Margaret Becker.
            p.   cm.
        ISBN 1-56507-847-0
        1. Devotional literature.   2. Becker, Margaret. 1959- .   I. Title.
    BV4832.2.B368   1998
    242--dc21   98-4078
                                                                       CIP

Design and Production by Koechel Peterson & Associates,
Minneapolis, Minnesota

To my mother,

PEGGY AUSTIN

Acknowledgements

My thanks to
HOLLY HALVERSON
and
DAVID McCRACKEN

Contents

Introduction

I've kept a journal since the age of eight. Though there was not much noteworthy happening in my eighth year, the habit of entering events and observations turned out to be a exercise that would mold the rest of my life.

I've been a professional writer now for 14 years, but my genre of choice has been songs. Each time I've had to creatively figure out a way to delicately place a "meaningful" thought, which might have taken years to form, into a three-and-a-half minute aural setting, complete with a musical "hook." It's not too easy and, at times, very constrictive. Hence, my need to write in a journal. There I can take all the time in the world to get my point across, and every other line doesn't have to rhyme—a considerable luxury for me. The results of the writings I've been jotting down for years have formed this book.

Each of the pieces that I've chosen to
include was cathartic for me. I've lived through
them. It was in their original transcription that
I saw myself in a "true light," sometimes flat-
tering, sometimes telling. This light is the light
I travel by—the light of faith.

It's been a journey to a "window" of
sorts, a place to become an active observer
of my own progression in this refining process
we call life. I'm trying to sit at this window
more often. I've seen simple things there,
things that remind me of my own time
line and my responsibility to plumb every
moment for its deepest gifts, whether the
reckless laughter of friends or the comfort
of a simple touch.

I want to recognize the truth in
my moments—recognize and feel it all
while it is living and breathing right in
front of me. I don't want to miss even one,

INTRODUCTION

because I believe that is all I have—all any of us truly have on this earth—the present moment.

I hope that by reading along with me, watching me peer into things both fearful and comforting, that you will gather treasures that you can employ to mark your own road. It is my highest hope, in fact, to leave the imprint of peace, the kind that remains steady in every circumstance. The kind that is eternal. The kind that passes all understanding.

I submit my journey to you in that spirit, and pray an extra measure of grace as you hold it up to your own.

Margaret Becker

I sit

in thick sweaters

at the

water's edge,

soothed by the endle

THAT

ombinations of the folding surf. ■

**I keep a
promise
to myself**

to view every

sunrise and

every sunset.

I sit in the rattan chair, white terry cloth robe bundled around me. It is daybreak of Christmas Eve. My feet and face are chilled by the crisp Gulf breeze flowing through the open French doors. It is the first moment of my awakening.

I stare into the sun as it lifts off the black-green ocean. I know it is too cold to sit like this, no coat or shoes, but I am chilled already in so many ways. It is familiar to me.

MARGARET
B E C K E R

Ennio Morricone's *Mission* plays softly in the background as I watch pelicans fall seaward, their beaks pointed like spears at their breakfast. To the left of them, dolphins arc into the sky, slick gray fins flashing Morse code messages, shouting of other life cycles being played out.

I gulp down deep breaths of icy air. These are long, luxurious, unhurried breaths, driving the present moment into my innermost recesses.

Tints and textures melt into a recognizable scene, a beautiful portrait coming into focus after a long sleep. I've been dormant for quite some time now, derailed by the act of living itself. *Frozen, encumbered.* Gummed with goals. Paranoid with purpose. As the morning's shades rise I realize that I've seen only gravel and dirt for the last eight years;

focusing on the placement of my own steps before they struck the ground, I tuned out all else.

Touch, beauty, and simple pleasures arrayed in constellations wept as I passed during those days, crying to be noticed and valued. I'm sure of it now as I close my eyes and attempt to escape the endless reams of paper chatter in my mind.

I've come to this house to right myself in life, to wake up, to rest. I've come to leave the wheel for a moment and assess my need of it. I've come here because had I refused, I believe I might have blinked and missed another decade. I fight now at the open door to keep my moist eyes wide to the fresh wind.

It is my first day without the phone, the fax, the deadline, and the doorbell. Only my family knows where I am, and at the end of my visit here, they will come collect me and find a sprinkling of freckles and a quieted soul.

I lay silent in the first part of my visit. I sit in thick sweaters at the water's edge, soothed by the endless combinations of the folding surf. I keep a promise to myself to view every sunrise and every sunset. They become a personal art gallery, open all hours, glorious vistas offering insights into the Creator's soul. I marvel daily at His technique.

I spend my days walking, running, sitting, addressing the things I've put in the "later" category for years now. I speak to seagulls and witnesses unseen. I watch two hurricanes slide down the glass walls of the back side of this house, the angry tempest softened into a Monet canvas with each droplet.

Layer by layer, my callused edges crack and fall, returning to the sand. The stress dreams cease waking me up. The tasks left undone leave my mind and return to the workplace. I begin to air out. I start to hear . . . things. Wonderful things— symphonies in the surf. And my own inner voice, weak and scratchy from disuse. I am surprised by it, by the things it wants to draw attention to.

Weeks into the visit I begin constructing the life I've yet to live, from the center outward, and I start with the cog of my existence—the center of my comfort— my faith. My belief in another dimension, another justice, another King, another government devoid of fallibility. My belief

in a place where mercy reigns supreme and

thoughtful, demonstrative, detailed love is expressed in microscopic ways.

On my knees during one sunset, I am gifted with a glimpse into that place. Overcome with my frailty, my insignificance in the eternal pattern of things, I say quietly, "I believe. I believe in that place, in the power that created this window to it."

And I do believe, because on some days—on good days—when my friends and family send reckless laughter through my house, I think I hear that place. When I watch a stranger's face soften at a polite gesture, I think we meet on that soil. And on the hard days, when my stomach fills with lead and tragedy is truly tragedy, I return to the laws of that place: all things work together for the good. And I consider its time line, time enough to repair. Endless days to bind together that which has been torn apart.

I am convinced of it. Not because someone told me to be. Not because I saw or heard something that persuaded my heart, although many things bear witness. But because when I tilt my head back in the sunlight and consider the number of my days, the very center of my being pulls me inward to a hidden world—an hourglass of sorts, wide, then painfully narrow, then wide again.

Music played. Delicate and sparkly, like icicles dropping on tiny chimes. Ting, ting, ting— all in ambient succession. My senses folded into it, in tiny gentle waves. Retreat.

15

I am deposited into a cavern of warmth.
A world where all the stars align and truth is
true. A place where the atomic energy of my
mind settles into the hum of a perfect mathe-
matical picture. Where my fingers stretch
wide in the air, feeling electricity dance on
their tips. It is the true center of breath.
The true sphere of life.

And I know, because I know, because
I know—against all else, I know.

MARGARET
BECKER

This is the world of the soul. The
world of the Spirit. The world we knew
before our flesh felt air. The world we fear
and seek; the world we disavow and embrace.
The world that propels us outward and
suctions us back, all in its good time, all
without our permission. We belong to it,
expatriates and nationals alike. It lays claim
to us, and somewhere within us, its deposit
will always bear witness to that fact.

It is against this world that I hold up
the fabric of my existence. It is like cheese-
cloth, diaphanous, textured with life. It acts
as a filter to soften the brilliance of the other
world. My eyes would be burned to white
without some substance separating me from
the sight. It is too magnificent.

I hold it there and consider its
vulnerability. Only porous skin. Only a

I hold it
there and
consider its
vulnerability.

heart beating in a bag of water, beating for reasons even the most learned don't understand. *For what purpose? To what end, this breath?* And when that beating ceases, what becomes of these thoughts— these thoughts that are heard only by unseen worlds?

So much more to consider than the rhythm of my own steps. I begin there. I count it a gift to build upon so dynamic a foundation.

I leave the voices behind. The yeas and nays—their roaring reduced to the soft squeaking of mice. I wait peacefully, day and night, and watch my road illuminate before me. Tiny street lights come to life, marking a way. The close-in focus, the half-century fuzzy but still recognizable.

This way is for the brave. It ignores the values culture has pressed into its hand. It escapes the collar of expectations held out by other travelers. It is littered with kindness and conviction. It allows God to be God. It expects Him to move, but not to fit.

This road is meted out to me in small segments, and with each I am afforded the opportunity to shrink from the call. There are other roads, but none seem as well fitted to all that dreams within me.

I step forward to answer the call of my first segment: Speak the truth as you have tasted it. Sow the love as you have reaped it. Reach up and paint what the eye cannot see—the visions of the soul—with bright, bold colors. Be brave and flamboyant in your strokes. No more looking from side to side. Number your days and find the joy hidden in each step.

On the last day, I stand at the shore, saying silent goodbyes. It is warmer now, and I mark the change. I am filled with purpose and a courage of the fully convinced, and yet my heart is soft to the touch. I am so filled that even the slightest addition overflows me, and I brim up with tears. Too much grace. Too much mercy. Too much peace, all running in fresh streams from that place.

We were sisters there

in our tiny

suburban

front yard,

sisters both bound and separated

20

THE FATE OF

**by
genetics and
circumstance.**

We were

fragile

and tough.

THE FRAGILE

Although I'm not sure how I first understood it, I knew she was fragile, and that in all things she must come first.

I think I sensed it innately as a child because perhaps as children we're more open to those merciful instincts that play across our consciences. Or maybe it's just that I saw the way other people treated her, like a beautiful porcelain doll, valuable and lovely, but not for play. I knew it then as well as I know it now: My developmentally disabled sister, Janie, was not weak or feeble, but fragile.

Even as a child, I strained with all my senses to feel what Janie felt. I wanted to see through her eyes. I wanted to know her beyond what she could tell me. Her disability left her without speech, so my task of "knowing" became wholly centered in nuance. I tried to unravel every mysterious expression, every response or lack of one to the surrounding world. I watched intently, from my emotions outward, trying to trace the edges of her being. I wanted to know her the way I knew my other siblings: what made her angry, what made her smile, what were her limits of tolerance. And once I learned them, I wanted to protect them, cater to them, and in some younger sister way, perhaps push them. Not in the way most kids do, out of spite, but rather with affection. I wanted to hug her, stroke her silky black hair, hold her hand, and skip down the driveway . . . all seemingly against her will.

Janie seemed unaware of me most of the time, or perhaps just indifferent. I'm sure that some of it had to do with the fact that I was the "new kid" in her world—draining all the attention she had become accustomed to. That was reason enough. But it was more than that. She was refused entry into the outside world because she didn't have the abilities to communicate with it. She retreated inward, searching for distractions and stimulus, reaching for what we all take for granted: the small evidences of being alive. I was part of the outside, an unwilling exile— but undaunted in my youthful energy.

I would try with all the resources I had.

From the beginning, Janie's delight was my delight. I wanted her to be happy. It was the most direct way to get into her world—making her content. I started with what I knew: the things that made me happy, like being first. I learned early how to stand back when we'd hear the rumble of my father's jeep in the evening. I knew to allow her to run ahead of me when he emerged from behind the squeaky green door, black lunch box in hand. After a long day's work, he smelled of wind and of sweat dried to a salt. And although I believe my father was dreaming of an ice-cold beer and a long shower, his attentions lay solely on us in those first moments of his free evening.

It was against the backdrop of my father's half-crouched body that I remember seeing a smile slowly emerge on Janie's face. Sometimes it was her only smile of the day.

On those nights my father played a friendly stalker, his Frankensteinesque strides making me flush with nervous anticipation. Shifting from foot to foot, Janie and I would jitter and dance with delight, our hands up to our faces. Fingers spread wide, we hid our tangled smiles. We awaited the familiar danger of the chase that was coming.

My father's growls were punctuated with laughter as he lumbered toward Janie. Her guttural giggling trailed behind her as she dragged her feet, always remaining close enough to catch. Several trips around the yard later, my father would snatch her into his arms and rub the tiny bristles of his five o'clock shadow against her creamy white Irish skin. Squirming happily in her yellow sunsuit, she'd wriggle away with a backward glance and assume her "catch me" stance, ready for more. This was a ritual, and when Janie was through, I was next.

We understood it. We reveled in it. We never acknowledged it to one another, but I knew we both felt it. Some things fragility cannot impede.

Sisters, both of us in our sunsuits; hers was always immaculate, mine always smeared with the long, brown dusty strokes of Long Island soil, the evidence of tomboy games and hide and seek. We were sisters in the chase there in our tiny suburban front yard, sisters both bound and separated by genetics and circumstance. We were fragile and tough, stubborn for reasons all our own. There where the friendly stalker made our laughter resound wildly through the streets, blood reigned and we were one on some plane. She was mine and I would protect her.

I saw her the last time I visited New York, her gray-green eyes almost luminescent against her milky skin as she spied the Christmas gift in my hand. Her hair was still that thick black Irish color, but now there were a few strands of gray interwoven, reminding me that time struggles to mark even the fragile. Still, I was amazed again at how smooth and unlined her face

I don't belong in this line anymore. I sense it—know it, even. But where to go? Which way? I wait in the puddles, rain, and my own tears... wait for—something. I know it will come.

TWO
THE FATE OF THE FRAGILE

was. I considered our faces, so similar; mine, and the litany of powders and creams I employ to hold back time's advances, hers, seemingly unmarred. There, settled in her group home, it seemed that what abilities birth had withheld, life had recompensed with poetic justice. I felt jealous of the peace she seemed to possess. It was the peace which so desperately eluded me; the art of living in immediacy.

Janie doesn't hold onto meaningless things. When she is disappointed, it is known. She expresses it, expelling all its bitter trappings from her soul. In the expression, it's eradicated. There is no such thing as a grudge in her world, no fertile ground for enmity between friends. All things are worked out as they happen. Emotional honesty abounds and the need to hide is eliminated. Janie has never learned the deceptive art of saying one thing yet meaning another. For her, etiquettes are basic and true. The niceties are functional, not seductive tools of acquiescence.

I suspect she never loses a night's sleep over what tomorrow may bring. Tomorrow is just there. It's an odd sort of justice, but one I don't begrudge. I muse that perhaps Janie is not the fragile one after all.

I muse that
perhaps Janie
is not the
fragile one
after all.

Aren't I the one who has everything, clutching it so tightly for fear of dropping one strand? Am I not the one who can snap out an agitated word at the slightest inconvenience, feeling justified because I've allowed so many other hurtful things to go unsaid? Isn't it I who must leave the television on at night to keep anxiety at bay so I can grasp a few hours' sleep? Suspicious, calculating, afraid to face things head on: am I not the truly fragile one?

I consider this, and then myself. I realize again that Janie is first. Not because of my allowances this time, but by nature of circumstance. She already has the fabric of life that I yearn for. I think she's had it all along.

Janie has made her peace. She has ordered her world as much as it will allow. A thread of acceptance in all things is woven throughout both the good and the bad. It forms a tapestry with odd color pairings and mismatched patterns, which at first seems incongruent. Upon deeper reflection, though, the work reveals a sage beauty— the beauty of the simple, of the fragile. In my eyes, it graces her with the wisdom of the older sister. And although she doesn't verbally offer its shelter to me, I commit it to memory and humbly take the warmth of it with me as if she herself had protectively placed it on my shoulders.

I am hers and she is mine. I am wordless in her shadow, and this too is the fate of the fragile.

TWO
THE FATE
OF THE
FRAGILE

We feasted there,

finding the courage

to look one another in the eye

for the first time

that day—

BERNIE'S

he way friends do—unafraid,

sharing
the
bread
of
humor,

TREASURE

knowing

each other

just a

tiny bit better.

We'd traveled all morning, bouncing around like marbles in one of those push-toys toddlers love. Minimalist stone and clay trails were the only route to our destination but they didn't faze our driver, Atmas. He sped along as if on pristine blacktop.

Ghana talk radio was blaring, reverberating in measured woofs off the steel panels of the truck. Between the rattling and the radio, our voices sounded like the bleating of sheep. Two turns into the journey, we were exhausted.

Atmas shared the front of the truck with my friend Bernie, a freelance writer by trade, a free spirit by nature. My manager Marc and I held the sway straps over either door as we vibrated in the back. We'd been driving for seven hours, although according to Atmas, it was only "two," which he punctuated by holding up two fingers the last three times we'd asked.

We were on our way to view some World Vision projects, hoping to see how this world-hunger relief agency was helping Ghana to fortify its villages against sickness and starvation. Bernie was there to chronicle the adventure.

Whether it was Bernie's appetite for true experience or just sheer boredom,

I'm not sure, but in the second "two"-hour segment, I watched her leave cultural sensitivity instruction behind and begin her great adventure. Bernie was in Africa, and she was going to experience it in all its fullness—no matter what.

She began with Atmas. She questioned him about the terrain . . . the projects . . . his family. But the language barrier kept ending in a frustrated "Aaay?" Determined to glean memories, Bernie finally got him to turn off the radio, and with an authority that surprised us all, she took out a three-dollar tin flute she bought at a souvenir shop in Ireland. "I will play you a song, Atmas," she declared as if he'd asked. Marc and I giggled coyly in the back with our heads lowered. We'd been on these trips several times now, and neither of us had made near the leap Bernie was making now.

"Hmmmm, what shall I play? Oh! I know! This is a popular American classic." Turning to us she added, "See if you know it."

It took us at least eight notes, but it was no secret. Our classic? "Knock Three Times on the Ceiling." Marc and I were miserable with movement, laughing as hard as we could without needing a neck adjustment. Leaning against the window,

I noticed the midday sun made the panes hot to the touch, even though we had the air conditioning on full blast.

Soon thereafter I was never more happy to hear downshifting as we pulled up, hours late, to our village. A brightly colored patch from a distance, the entire populace of this small community sat in the only unshaded area in sight—the village center—in what was undoubtedly their Sunday best. Layers upon layers of African fabrics and headdresses, languishing there like a multicolored puddle in the sun . . . until they saw us.

Startled by our arrival, they jumped to life, taking their places in a formal procession. Native music began. The women formed a soulful conga line, dancing and singing as they snaked their way around the few chairs that the men sat in. A choir of children with voices ringing out like harmonized chimes added to the surreal cultural wash. The entire sight, resplendent with the sense of community, was a gift of substance, *a gift that made room for itself in my jangled heart.*

Bernie was touched, too, so much so that we'd barely stopped the truck when she leaped from the front seat, running ahead of us all—straight toward the conga line. Affixing herself squarely on the end, she pulled out her Kleenex and began emulating the lithe waving motions of the other women. In her khaki shorts, with her baseball hat cocked slightly to one side like a retired fisherman's, she was a sight. Heads turned. The proceedings continued, but all eyes were on Bernie. Including mine.

There was that moment when strangers strain to sense the intent, the hidden meaning of an action. I felt a collective holding of the breath, but it passed quickly when the children began giggling. This was reckless abandonment—the lack of self-consciousness we all dream of possessing, no matter what the culture. In all of our own ways, we recognized and respected it.

Greetings completed, we moved as a group throughout the various phases of life in the village. At the "cocoa nut" presentation, Bernie was all but kidnapped by the village women. Completely charmed by her boldness, they kept her with them for the rest of the visit.

We went on. Fresh water, recycling produce, sewing clothes—so many seemingly small adjustments were bringing such bounty to this remote place. All the works in progress

*Our eyes met, and
I recognized him.
Taking my pointer
finger in his tiny
grasp, he led me
to the flashing
evergreen.
We stood there
watching the
rhythmic patter
of the lights.*

that we saw that afternoon brought stability
and sustenance to these people.

When our visit drew to a close,
our interpreter instructed us to return to
the clearing for the customary send-off.
Back to the chairs we walked in the hot
sun, only this time they were set up in two
parallel lines with 25 feet between them.
Our party took one side; the king and
queen and their court, the other. Our
guide told us that the royals never address
strangers directly, nor should we address
them. It was a sign of respect.

We sat in silence. I studied the
ground, mentally tracing the sweat that ran
in lines down the backs of my calves. No one
looked at anyone else. My guide assured me
this was normal. Just physically sitting in
proximity here was considered visiting.

The calm broke when a woman's
voice called out—in something between
a melody and a bellow—"Friend!"

Whispering rustled everywhere.
Marc and I stared at one another. "Was that
the queen?" I asked. "Did she say, 'friend'?
Are you her friend? 'Cause I know I'm not."

"Me either," he answered. We
both turned to Bernie, whose smile at that
moment could have swallowed the entire

world. One lone pointer finger resting on her chest said it all. Excitedly she stood up and whispered, "I think she means me!"

We tried to stop her—to confirm that she should approach the king and queen—but she paid no attention. Dust followed her as she quickly traversed the span, bowing her head the whole way.

I think I saw the queen smile as Bernie approached, although she didn't look her way. The only indication of any exchange between them was the laughter of the people seated closest. Moments later Bernie returned to us in a trance. Digging singlemindedly through her backpack, she acknowledged none of our questions. We too were silenced when we saw her take out a pen and—the tin whistle.

The large green letters spelling "Ireland" on the side sent a ripple of laughter through the people. In theater voice Bernie began, "Oh, great queen. You have requested that I become your pen pal, an honor that I gratefully accept. I am a writer by trade and this is my favorite pen. I present it to you now as a gift. I will never forget you and your beautiful village. You are rich beyond measure with your sense of community and love. *I've been moved.*"

He spoke to me in a language I don't yet know. The room was silent but for our soft banter.

Tom's mother whispered, "See, I told you."

—Christmas in Brooklyn

With that, the queen finally looked at Bernie directly, taking the pen from her hand.

"And now," Bernie continued as she led a 360-degree sweep addressing us all, "I will play you a classic American song on my flute."

"No!" Marc and I hissed, crouching down. "Please," we asked, half in prayer, "not 'Knock Three Times on the Ceiling'!" We closed our eyes, dreading the downbeat.

What ensued was a jazz-odyssey rendition of "Amazing Grace," riddled with high-spirited, breathless sonic spikes and skews . . . not indigenous to the original melody. Eyes shot from left to right, hands quickly drawing to faces. The wave of laughter became a grand host, bidding us closer to another, offering commonality as the main course.

We feasted there, finding the courage to look one another in the eye for the first time that day—the way friends do—unafraid, sharing the bread of humor, knowing each other just a tiny bit better.

Singularly, Bernie reminded two continents that there is little that truly separates us. *Ultimately we all laugh and cry in similar meter, no matter what the language.*

Song completed, Bernie barely sat once again when the conga line formed, signaling the end of our visit. I felt my throat tighten as she walked toward it and I saw the women break form, giving her place.

Marc and I made our way back to the truck. Although I couldn't see her, I knew Bernie wasn't far behind. Off in the distance I heard a chant growing closer: "Berr-nee, Berr-nee!" In a pod of people, arms loaded with cocoa soap and trinkets, Bernie made her final farewells.

"Berr-nee, don't forget to tell your friends about the soap. It makes the skin lovely to the touch!" called one new friend. "We will be happy to provide it to you!" she added with a wink.

Laughter and much excitement accompanied our truck as we pulled away. Children ran alongside as Bernie, the visiting emissary, cradled her soap and waved like a beauty queen.

When we could see them no longer, Bernie turned back to us. *"I will never forget this. This has been amazing."* As she wiped tears away, I noticed a beautiful, large, beaded bracelet dangling from her wrist.

"What's that?"

"Oh," she said through an enchanted smile, "it's the queen's bracelet. She gave it to me before I got in the truck."

All I could do was shake my head and wonder what it's like to be so free . . . so brave . . . so alive. I took note and prayed for the spell of life to fall upon me in such irresistible swells. I watched her pack her gifts into her bag and I pined for Bernie's treasure.

"But you knew

he didn't love me—

didn't you?"

*She smiled the
way people smile*

**when
they
are
about
to cry.**

chapter
four

It was deep and brave,

trembling with the full

knowledge of pain.

WISHES OF
INNOCENTS

He smiled, his mouth crinkling in all the right places, but falling short of his eyes. He didn't love her. He loved what he saw, but not what he didn't see.

There was another boy who smiled at her, clear through to all the places that mattered. Even his curly black hair shifted back at the very top when he grinned her way, but she didn't want him. She wanted Ed. Ed was "the one."

Too young to understand when to hold my tongue, I asked her, "Why do you want to marry him so intensely? You're only 23. There's lots of time. He doesn't treat you right." But she was weeping. She wouldn't look at me. He'd been ignoring her lately, and even kissed another girl for all the world to see. Still, Patty would hear none of it. It was Eddie. The questions she asked were not the same as mine. Hers were those of a spurned heart: Why was he ignoring the obvious? When would he come around?

I watched Patty cry until I thought my heart would burst. She took no comfort from any of us standing by. I wanted to punch Eddie's pudgy nose. I think Patty knew, and in an act of premature loyalty, she asked us all to go away—especially me. On the way out the door I asked her sister Joan, "Why is she so stuck on marrying Eddie?"

"She believes that he is the one that God has chosen for her. And really, I don't think we should interfere, Margaret. We don't know. Only she does."

I studied Joan's eyes, the same flashing blue with brown specks that Patty had. Was she convinced? Did she agree? No—maybe not convinced, but blood she was and as such, she would stand firm.

Maybe I was crazy. Maybe I just didn't understand the ways of "spiritual romance," but it didn't feel right to me. When people stand in the newness of love, fresh and expectant, crying and anguish weren't supposed to be part of it—were they?

I had weeks to consider it as Eddie came to his senses. Something apparently summoned him once again into Patty's backyard, where a good-night kiss turned into a mutual decision, and the wheel of fate turned forward a notch or two.

My words to Pat still hung in the air between us, a foul curtain somewhere between an insult and a betrayal. I wanted to slash those words to ribbons—find a flamethrower and blast them from existence. But I said them. She heard them. And that was that.

She forgave me, though. She must have because we never spoke of the incident again. And when the date was set, Patty chose me to stand with her and her family, a witness to the event.

It was a year of many marriages at that church, her two sisters' among them. It was like a love mist settled on the congregation; fairy dust falling in open eyes, making the common seem grand and the passable, outstanding. Everyone I knew was getting married. So far-reaching was the bliss that those of us the spell escaped were ushered headlong into its tailwind by the affected.

These were the motivations behind the dinner at Chi-Chi's with Pat, myself, Eddie, and Jed: the mountain man 15 years my senior, and—perhaps—my newly intended. Pat chattered breathlessly, "You'll like him. He's got a great heart. Really loves the Lord! He's got a cabin in the woods, good job at the power plant . . . give it a chance."

Patty didn't tell me about his mountain dialect nor did Ed tell him about my New York aversion to pronouncing "r's." Our conversation fumbled at every turn. It was an entire evening of "'Scuse me?" and "Wha?" I couldn't even read his lips through his long, gray beard.

I went home sick to my stomach. I doubted my world, my ability to hear. I questioned my place in this new spiritual culture. All for about 24 hours, and then my inner compass kicked in. I recoiled from the concept of love for love's sake, marriage for the sake of being married and making everyone else feel better about my life. Or even worse, because it is what the masses do. I heard my mother's voice: "I married your father because I couldn't stand to be without him. Never settle for less."

I wouldn't, I decided, even if it made me an outcast of sorts. I'd sustain the concerned whispers: "Oh, you know that she was one of the ones that didn't get asked. If you ask me, I think it was that accent. . . ."

I was happy, fulfilled. And God was big enough to open my eyes to Jed, or any other guy for that matter. But I wanted to leave it to Him.

I continued on, as did Patty and Ed. I watched from a distance as their relationship met all the challenges that come when the veneer wears thin and you're standing face-to-face with either your best friend, or a stranger. Years passed. They didn't make it. And not for lack of trying, either. Certainly not for lack of support or

I squirmed
in the silence,
searching for
a truth.

prayer. I watched them struggle with all the usual issues and then the extra ones that come along with a belief system like the one that joined them together. They bent. They patched. But it crumbled.

Toward the end, Patty and I walked down the water line on an Atlantic beach.

"Did you ever think it would end this way, Mag?"

I hesitated, remembering the acidic wall of words that separated us once. Older, hopefully wiser, I squirmed in the silence, searching for a truth.

"Well?" she pressed, looking at me, eyes gleaming.

I studied the sand. "It's not important how I thought things would go, is it? It's not my life—it's yours. Maybe you and Ed would be best served if everyone around you would shut up and let you guys sort it out for yourselves."

She stopped walking, causing me to do the same. She spoke to my ear while I watched the seagulls. "Margaret, there was a time when I wanted your silence. Now I need your words." Demanding my candor, she persisted. "Did you know?"

Lightning bolts cracked in my brain, split-second decisions flashing. I scrambled,

*Transition.
The dance of the
soul and spirit,
finally emerging
right in the
true world.*

landing on all fours at the door of risk. "No, I didn't know. I thought I knew, but I didn't. I'd hoped for better for both of you. I prayed, stood with you. I still do.

"I've had many theories about what took place in that year you guys got married. I'm not sure about a lot of it. But I really don't know why your union didn't make it and others did, and to speculate would be foolish."

We began walking again. "I don't understand it, Patty, but I am here for you." I placed my hand on her shoulder and noticed the mark of the sun on her cheek. "Whatever you need—I'm here."

We walked on. She let out a tiny, ironic laugh, followed by a tear. "When did you get so spiritual and politically correct?"

"I don't want to say something I'll regret. I'm inexperienced in these things." *I meant it.*

"But you knew he didn't love me—didn't you?" She smiled the way people smile when they are about to cry. It was deep and brave, trembling with the full knowledge of pain.

I looked directly at my friend, and deep into her. "Yes. I knew. I hoped that he would fall in love with you along the way—that was my consolation."

We didn't speak for the next 20 minutes down to the Crab Shack, nor the 20 minutes back. I thought of how this love challenged my value system both at its inception and now, at its dissolution. I thought of how I had no right to pass judgment on either process.

When we finally sat, observing the sun dropping quickly into the rough sea, Patty turned to me, one eye squinted. "How did you know, Margaret?"

I sat there, wishing I had a deeper answer—something psychological and brilliant. I gave the only response I had. "His eyes didn't smile when he looked at you."

To my surprise she turned back to the orange circle, now half-obscured. "I know," she replied.

She looks more

beautiful to me

than she ever

has before.

DEEP
BLUE

**The
lines
on her
face**

have fallen

to her fitly,

*tracing the joy
and the kindness*

she has

expressed

over the years.

My father and I are waiting in my mother's hospital room. She is sleeping. An old Navy comedy crackles on the television. We sit in tan vinyl chairs, chins up to face the elevated monitor. Take-out containers sit half open before us on the food tray, cafeteria sandwiches half eaten. We wait.

Like an animal, I pace the cage. Inwardly I walk back and forth, unable to turn my attention from the source of my rage: this suffering. Who allowed it? Who caused it? Who is responsible and how can I make him or her pay? *How helpless I feel, how angry. I have no target.*

I am nauseated, bloated with empty energy that sickens me. Like hot air pumped into my soul, its force expands me. I billow but I don't gain—I don't glean any tools with which to deal with this situation.

I hold my mother's hand as I have on and off all day. I am drawn to it, hoping on some plane it will act as a conductor, funneling my energies into her, bolstering her body. Hers is a small hand, strong and utilitarian; rich with work. How foreign other women's hands seemed to me as a child—pampered and manicured with long, shiny red nails. No garden-soil smudges, no crags and nicks, no freckles and lines.

It's a creative hand, with an eloquence for ushering lives across the years. I rehearse its history as I cradle it: the firm hand that held mine tightly, its power almost levitating me across the city street. The lined hand that lovingly moved my own while teaching me how to crochet. Of late, the thin, opaque hand that frequently reaches for mine, unbidden, for reasons I don't know—perhaps just to feel.

She sleeps. I pray, and hope, and wish. And believe. Try to believe . . . until I get angry and start pacing again.

The room is tiny. We are compressed in here, sickness and health pushed together, one unit of sorts, seeking balance at every turn. White on white, rough sheets against cold skin. The bed is too high or this chair is too low. I can't get the vantage point I want. I want to see her, watch her chest rise and fall in slight increments. I want her to see me when she wakes.

I position myself near the tiny rectangular window that lays the afternoon sun across her face. I study her under its scrutiny and fully expect to see the gray pallor that surgery leaves; a fragile woman who dangles in the fist of fate. I steel myself against it and all the new fears it will ignite.

But she looks more beautiful to me than she ever has before. The lines on her

FIVE
DEEP BLUE

Bursting through the surface, eyes wide through the process. Blasting long-held breaths of transition from her lungs; spraying a fine mist of diamonds into the air. I saw it over months, it happened, and she was treading now.

I am
looking at her
very soul.

face have fallen to her fitly, tracing the joy
and the kindness she has expressed over the
years. Like passionate artwork, her countenance
is a meticulously crafted sculpture, perfectly
aligned and displayed. It lacks nothing.

I brush her hair back with my hand
and am startled when her clear blue eyes
flash open, meeting my own with neither
fear nor dullness. The light pierces them,
plumbing their clarity. I am speechless at
the first impression they afford me—their
youth, their will, the fighter they embody.

It's as if everything around us, right
up to the rims of her irises, dissipates into an
indistinct color wash. The television sounds
like gibberish folded into a distant surf. The
sterile clank and shuffle of stainless steel
hospital equipment in the hallway sound like
pins dropping on pillows. Her soft breathing
is reminiscent of rushing winds. All I see, all
I hear is her. The depths of her. The source of
her. I am looking at her very soul.

I am stunned. The stark beauty
silences the choir of angst that has haunted
my thoughts. I dare not look away. If there
were a shade of blue more devastating in
its magnificence, I have not seen it. If there
were a life force more brilliant in its emi-
nence, I have not encountered it.

In the moment, I feel a film of familiarity melt from my understanding and I realize how all these years I have been watching her theatrically fulfill her various roles. The face changed, the posture, the trimmings and baubles, but never the essence. It was all props and grease paint.

In that deep blue she meets me. She emerges, only a girl. All this time . . . only a girl.

MARGARET
BECKER

Nothing matters now except that the girl feels the force of love that surrounds her. It is the eternal glue that binds life in all dimensions together. It permeates this room, floating around us invisibly, without fanfare. *I want her to be cradled in it.*

The anger, the angst, require too much energy now. Sharpened by the blades of suffering, I am honed, beginning love's unveiling with a new precision. It demands all of me, and I give it happily.

MOSAIC IN MOTION

The scene blurs in front of me,

as if I watch

from underwater.

These are the harmonies
of their blood.

They've
learned
them

in equal

measures

as children.

A simple brown barn with walls made of common materials, out in the middle of nowhere. Stone, thatch, and wood form an airy edifice, today filled with young lives; wild dreamers sustained by belief and promise.

I stand, a voyeur, at the back. There is a warmth here I did not expect; an acceptance I haven't seen anywhere else in this country. An ease. I was told not to hope for this when I arrived in South Africa. Apartheid was newly disassembled, and there were warnings about not expecting too much. It would take years for true and lasting change to occur.

I have tried not to expect, but I am unsuccessful. The "blacks only" eating sections at restaurants, the lingering disdain for physical proximity—it still jolts me. I don't want to judge, only to hurry the process along in my little sphere of influence. That's why I act as if I don't see the signs, why I greet my dear black friend Buster, onstage in front of 2,000 people, with a kiss, why I let the silence shame when bigoted jokes are told. I am a guest in this culture. I am not invited to comment, only to perform. And frankly, I have no right to comment. These are not my streets that are straining to move in the proper directions.

I am not
invited to
comment, only
to perform.

The barn, though; it is my sedative.
It is filled with a generation in the throes of questioning. It is the chapter in most kids' lives that parents dread: "Why must I do as you do? Why must I believe what you do?" They are frightening questions that precede potentially disastrous decisions. Those of us who watch stand trembling, only hoping that somewhere in each heart there is a plumb line of definition with a magnet attached: something to pull each kid back to the ideals and morals that he can live by with full conviction and safety.

This is a Youth For Christ retreat, and I am here to sing. My time is drawing near when one of the leaders asks for the audience to settle so he can start the night with prayer. Up until that point, it had been hard to see defined cliques or circles. There was too much movement. But when the call for prayer came, I was sure that the mosaic would align itself in some partisan pattern of color.

I was wrong. The group drops to the floor in one mass. Speckled and messy with disregard, the Zulus sit next to the Dutch Afrikaans, who sit next to the Blacks, who sit next to the Belgians. There are no distinguishable lines. No one seems uncomfortable.

A small stream of prayer requests begins. The usual: sick relative, unemployed parents, direction . . . and the one that pleads the emergence of a new day. A white Afrikaans girl struggles to her feet. "I'd like prayer for my father. He is a policeman and he has been cruel to many of your fathers. For that I ask your forgiveness. I never believed as he does. My request is for him. He is struggling to accept the new order of things. He doesn't like it, but I believe in my heart that he is a good man and God can help him see the truth—that we are all brothers and sisters. Please pray for my father." By the end of her words she is choking on tears. She sits down and buries her face in her friend's neck. The room is mute with emotion. A short moment passes.

Another girl stands, this one black. "My name is Saysha and I'm from Soweto. My father has been beaten and he is bitter. He cannot forgive the oppressions." Squarely facing the first girl she continues, "I forgive your father, and his father. I forgive. You are my sister. Let's pray for our parents, that they can learn to forgive one another—and themselves."

The words stand like new steel: untarnished, thudding with the promise of strength, waiting to be inserted into the structure of a new bridge.

Love. Light.
I heard nothing
but the distant
crystalline chimes.
Further now, but
friendly; speaking
of other worlds...
other beauties.

MARGARET
BECKER

Many cry now, slowly taking one another's hands. A tentative chain forms. Pockets of kids—just children—rise to their feet, some with arms encircled round each other. **Patches of white and black blend into one unified, multihued, granite rock.** Without prompt, they stand arrayed as one tribe, one nation, one strong resolution. *They will go a different way than their fathers, I think. They will hold different hands than their mothers held.* That night I see it clearly for all time: with them lies true abolition. This generation will bring it to bear.

Through the sniffling, one voice rises. A young boy sings a native church hymn, "Nkosi Sikelel' iAfrika"—a song seeking God's blessing and direction on South Africa—a song forbidden by law up until now because of its significance in Nelson Mandela's campaign for equality.

Nkosi, sikelel' iAfrika;

                Lord, bless Africa;

Malupakam' upondo Iwayo;

                May her horn rise up;

Yiva imitandazo yetu

                Hear Thou our prayers

Usiskelele.

                And bless us.

Like an army returning from war, from
hard-won battles fought for freedom and mercy,
the group fills the room with determined conviction. This boy leads a melodic march on time-
held cruelties. Although I share their reverence,
I can't bear to close my eyes with them. I want
to witness history groaning with change in
front of me. In a far corner I watch two adults,
a black man and a white woman, arms around
each other's shoulders, swaying, singing—tears
streaming down their faces.

The room bursts with brilliantly
arranged African harmonies, as every mouth
opens and closes in synchronism. It's breathtaking. The scene blurs in front of me, as
if I watch from underwater. These are the
harmonies of their blood. They've learned
them in equal measures as children. This
song is from their soil. It has no favorites,
no color codes. It belongs to them all.

They sway, arms entangled, eyes
closed, heads bowed. I wonder if I should
sway too, grab someone, envelop myself in
this glorious moment. *But I don't.* It is not
for me to participate. It does not belong to me.
They have earned it and by some divine gift,
I have been granted the privilege to witness it.
That is the extent of my involvement, yet it
feels bountiful to me.

The song comes to a hopeful conclusion, resonant with wisdom that reaches far beyond the collective years represented in the room. I watch as in my mind's eye the segregated, misshapen images begin to fade. The adult undercurrent of resistance to justice begins to lighten in the balance. And undeniably, this nation begins making quick progress against a lie that has ravaged their culture for decades. It will probably take a generation before its primary hold is broken, but as I look on in this simple brown barn, I am sure that these children are up to the task.

There was absolutely

nothing in my

one-bedroom

apartment—

nothing except

**the
three-
by-two
furry
rug.**

It was my bed,

my breakfast table,

the seat of honor

SOUP
AND
DREAMS

for

guests,

my prayer

mat....

65

Every day on my way to college, I passed it. Glowing orange in the sunlight, shouting of cute guys, white teeth, and adult freedom, the used 1973 Fiat Spyder convertible was the center of my new world. To me it was the symbol of the perfect adult life that awaited me out there somewhere.

My friend Sandy went with me to kick the tires. She was from Brooklyn and she could cut a deal. Her "take it or leave it" attitude got me $700 off the asking price and financing. I got into that cream puff and drove it off into the Southern sunset toward my new perfect life, all the way to Newport News, Virginia, where I was starting my post-college life. My new job? Assistant manager trainee at Radio Shack.

I took an apartment. That's what you do when you get out of college. All my belongings fit very nicely in my Fiat: my guitar, a few clothes, and a furry blue bathroom rug.

The first day I went to Wal-Mart. Cleaning supplies, one bowl, one spoon, one towel later, I balked. Twenty-eight dollars! I couldn't spare it. But then, how would I eat, or dry off? I made the leap into the icy waters of adult reality.

I drove home in my fancy car, looking like much more than I was, wondering why I'd rushed myself all these years to get here. This was going to be tough.

There was absolutely nothing in my one-bedroom apartment—nothing except the three-by-two furry rug. It was my bed, my breakfast table, the seat of honor for guests, my prayer mat. . . .

Friends would stop by to see my new "place." I was quite excited to show it off. But the response was always the same: I'd open the door with my warmest greetings and they'd be standing there, smiles quickly transforming into silent ohhh's. Peering from corner to corner and leaning in, they'd stammer, "My . . . are you moving out?" Or "Uh . . . your stuff hasn't arrived yet, I guess."

My Christian friends were the worst. Their comments were always followed by intrusive questions about my spiritual life. Was I praying? Did I "seek" God before I made the move? Were there hidden sins? Did the pastor know about this?

My answers were suspect. It was obvious by their penetrating stares that my friends thought I was either daft or just lying. They'd pray for me, they promised, always slipping in something about true repentance.

I was confused by them, frankly.
I had this old-fashioned notion of starting
from nothing and making something.
I didn't see where that was a sin.

My friend Jana surprised me once
when she brought over a clothes basket full of
food and utensils one night. With great care
she carried it into my kitchen, offering to put
the items away. Opening cabinets, affording
herself the unedited view of my life, she gasped.
Two cans of Campbell's tomato soup, and one
box of instant oatmeal. In the fridge—one
onion. One week's food allotment.

"There is something majorly wrong
in your life, Margaret," she said firmly.

"What? What do you mean? It's all
I need."

"But look at this. Look! You are
starving to death. And come out here . . .
into the living room. There is absolutely
nothing in this place. You are out of God's
will. And listen, you haven't been to church
in a few weeks. What is going on?"

"Nothing's going on, Jana. I'm
struggling right now to make ends meet.
I haven't been avoiding church, but I have
to work 80 hours a week to pay my bills.
I have responsibilities. I get to service when
I'm not scheduled."

I didn't see

where that

was a sin.

"But this can't be God. How can it?" She looked around at my empty place.

I disagreed. I'd proceeded here after receiving all the correct signs and markers. I had none of the luxuries, that was true, but I had all of the essentials: my faith, my Bible, my goals, my rug, and an ear to hear. God knew all of this. He got me my job and my home and the way I saw it, He would achieve something through it all; something hearty and lasting. Why shouldn't I go through this? I knew other people did. Was I exempt somehow?

Jana left, shaking her head. "You really should see the pastor, Margaret."

I already had, and he didn't seem too alarmed by it all. He'd had his share of lean times, too. But Jana was a good friend, a dear friend, and I considered her words. I prayed that if necessary, God would show me the error of my ways.

The months dragged on. Some days I was dizzy with hunger. Some days I would break for lunch at the food court in the mall, just to smell the fries. I'd pray that someone I knew would see me sitting there and offer to buy me something—anything.

Most of my friends stopped visiting my place, afraid my condition might be contagious.

Still I read, prayed, and wrote.

I listened, and heard many good things that have guided me over the years. I learned that I am a survivor. I learned how to be content with little, and how to recognize the bounty in small things. I received the unique treasure of fullness there in the midst of nothing.

I worked hard and eventually saved up enough to buy a chair and another cup.

I was riding high. Eventually I sensed that chapter coming to a close and I felt released to go on to the next thing.

Shortly before I left, a policeman from church asked me out on a date. Although I'd been admiring him from afar for months, in all honesty it was the prospect of a free meal that closed the deal. Steak . . . pasta. I knew it would be good. I salivated as I pictured how it would all unfold. Start off with a generous salad bar plate, then some soup, then some filet . . . ahhh. I couldn't wait.

I stood at the window that night, eagerly watching for car lights. I didn't want him to come in, didn't want to have to field the usual questions—just wanted to get right to the meal.

The car arrived. I ran out, locking the door behind me. He seemed exhausted when I climbed in.

"Wow, what a day. I hope you don't mind, Margaret, but it's been a tough one. I thought maybe we'd run to Denny's and come back to your place to watch some TV. I really don't feel like going somewhere fancy. Is that all right?"

No, it truly wasn't all right. I saw visions of stuffed whatever fading before my eyes, but we didn't know each other well enough for me to say so. Food was just food, after all. But I just didn't know how I was going to get out of the TV thing.

"Yeah. Umm . . . that's fine, Ricky. Just one thing, though; I'm not a big TV watcher. We could go back and just talk. How's that?"

"Well—yeah sure." He was a little confused but I was too hungry to work it out for him. Denny's was better than tomato soup, so off we went.

When Ricky pulled back into my driveway, I noticed the venetian blinds in my living room looked crooked. When his head-lights swept across them, I saw why. Someone had broken the window.

Ricky saw it, too. Alerted, almost in one motion he shut off the lights, turned off the ignition, and reached under his seat for his gun. His police radio clicked on, and police code began. Other units were on the way.

"You've been robbed, Mag. I'm going to investigate."

"But Rick, I don't think that you . . ." I started to laugh. I tried to tell him that the robber would have been sorely disappointed at his take. But I couldn't finish my sentence. I was laughing too hard.

"Now calm down, Margaret. It's natural to feel a shock when this sort of thing happens, but you need to calm down. I'll take care of it. Stay here."

"But Ri—" The door slammed and I was smiling. **What a fitting end to it all.**

Crouching stealthily, Rick made his way to the front door, which stood partially open. In classic police stance, he announced himself and kicked it back. I saw the shock on his face when he looked inside. He entered cautiously.

Taking deep breaths, trying to shake off the laughter that now seemed compounded because of the seeming seriousness of the situation, I got out of the car and traced his steps. He met me at the door, gun holstered, shaking his head in amazement. "I don't know how they did it, Margaret, but before you go in there, brace yourself—they got everything."

Maybe I didn't fully know, although on some level I suspect I did: because it was like static electricity in the air— little jolts of realization stinging me at unexpected junctures.

I felt the same inability to control my laughter that I'd had in the library many times, slouching behind some opened encyclopedia—everything seemed funny.

"They did?" I brushed Rick aside and entered the living room. There stood my chair, my blue furry rug, my Bible, and my guitar. Rick followed me to the kitchen, attempting to calm my giggling hysteria the whole way. Soup and onion, and place setting—all intact.

I caught my breath. "They got nothing, Rick. Absolutely nothing."

"Nothing?" He did the same sweep over my "belongings" I'd seen dozens of times now. "You've lived like this all this time?"

I nodded.

He looked at me hard. "You get enough to eat tonight? How about dessert?"

I left that city filled and looking just like what I was: someone in process, someone in transit, someone who was taken care of—enjoying the ride. And most of all, someone whose greatest treasures would always fit in a Fiat, *with room to spare*.

I shake myself

and say,

"This is it!

This is your life!

Taste it, smell it,

touch it,

feel it!

WAVES

Let these waves

pour down on you

like a welcome

spring rain."

As concerns rehearse themselves one by one in my mind, starting as fleeting thoughts and growing into full-blown tears, I get up, sleepless, to watch the ocean for a while.

The steady rhythm of the water is mesmerizing. Hypnotically, the small waves meld imperceptibly into one another. As I watch, their ferocity fades into the familiar and become no longer waves individual but rather a distant, singular motion that begins somewhere in Europe and ends at my window. I expect their end and I feel it in my chest: a barely audible low boom reverberates with each crash. *Their dance makes me think of aging.*

My own aging process is coming in waves. The first wrinkle—the first wave. So unfamiliar and jarring, that initial physical flaw, I almost convinced myself it was unique. Every day for a while I was fixated on it, checking to see if perhaps I'd made too much of it, or maybe that I was mistaken entirely about its existence. But the truth, belligerent and unchanging, reasserted itself and somewhere in my center, I knew I'd begun the journey—the journey that wasn't supposed to include me.

I struggled with it, knowing I too must travel the road of ripening, though I took some comfort in knowing that the part containing frail, white-haired people was still seemingly miles away. I resembled the people at the beginning of the road.

Sometimes I was even able to convince myself that the two roads didn't join.

But then there was the next evidence of passing time and my deterioration within it. . . and then the next. I watch the web of wrinkles emerging, hinting a ghostly premonition of the mask I'll don as I travel down the road. I sense the waves ahead: the small hindrances, the sprinkling of tiredness, the realization that I've been an adult longer than I was a child. Several waves down . . . the imploding sonic boom of the finite in my stomach.

The evidences that I am not immune blur into continual motion. In my soul, in my room, in my tiny world at three A.M., I'm watching my new face appear. *The waves wash away my denial, without any emotional ether to deaden the sense of loss.*

It's a furious circle, this muscular motion. I settle myself, knowing what I've suspected all along: I can't stand against it. Empowered by the truth, I resolve afresh to let it move me. I have no choice but to believe

I resembled
the people at
the beginning
of the road.

that somewhere there is a Divine rhythm to it all. "Move me," I hear my inward voice say with resolute calm. "Move me to live with a heightened sense of time slipping through my fingers." I don't want to turn around at the end and look back, regretful that I didn't take more chances, seize every opportunity, experience every moment of laughter, every hot tear. What is life if not to feel, to be changed by the experience of feeling?

I pray, beg for wisdom. Not the same wisdom I sought before the waves—laden with practicalities and Catholic schoolgirl adherence to the acceptable order of the world. This is different. What I want is the wisdom of the marked—the wisdom of the waves, where I move in harmony with life's current. The wisdom of living in the here and now, close to the skin where sharp edges draw blood and tenderness reverberates warmth. Where each breath is a precious gift. Where all the senses rise in symphony.

I shake myself and say, "This is it! This is your life! Taste it, smell it, touch it, feel it! Let these waves pour down on you like a welcome spring rain. Don't second-guess the minutiae: the unimportant cosmetics of everyday living . . . the inanimate 'things' of position and power . . . the hollow formalities

I feel as if I've been living in a bubble for years. I heard a truth and in my earnestness to honor it, I honored people, traditions, and values that perhaps were not honor-worthy.

EIGHT
WAVES

I am ready to hear a different voice, my own. It may be hard for even me to recognize, but I must try to find it. I must use it.

of expectation. Be reckless, even sloppy, about this passionate experience, this frightening thread of events that is called your life!" I pray God give me the grace to unfold the gift of each moment with the veracity of a six-year-old on Christmas morning.

As the first blueness of morning washes across the vista, I wonder what there is to fear. Death? I live and walk unwillingly toward death every moment of my life. No one can change that. So there is . . . nothing to be afraid of.

I lay back down in the crisp sheets and hold my position. I close my eyes and wonder what could be more important than experiencing the journey in its fullness. What could be more insulting to an eternal, loving God than not enjoying it? This is the proper way to treat the tiny amount of existence I've been allotted.

And as I drift, I realize that these thoughts come courtesy of the wrinkles. And the trade-off seems more than fair.

WHAT SHE KNOWS

She was speaking in a language

I didn't understand,

    but the camera captured

    the intent in her smile

in a language I did know.

**Kindness.
Simple
touch.**

Attention—

    valuable gifts of love

    tumbling from her

    every appendage.

*Puffs of light,
far away.
Blossoming
bursts trickling
to the grounds
in trails of
illuminated salt.*

"**D**at a man, Ms. Becker. He a man!"

"Who? Who is a man, Cecelia?" my sister questions her special education student.

"Him," she says, pointing. "Up there on a board!" My sister Katy turns to see a picture of Mother Teresa, their subject for the day. She chuckles.

"No, Cecelia. That's no man. That's a great woman, you just can't see her hair. We're going to learn about her today."

Cecelia knows what she knows. Under her breath, she says it again. "Dat a man."

Katy, a disenfranchised parochial school graduate, laughs as she shares it with me. When we catch our breath, she goes on to detail her great respect for Mother Teresa and her work. She explains why, in a backwoods town in Virginia, she chose to include her in the Real Life Basics course she'd quietly been teaching these high-school special-ed kids, instead of the standard curriculum.

"They need to know real things. How to balance a checkbook. How to make change at the store. How to go for a job interview—and whom to respect," Kate shares.

I agree. I remember the first time I saw an interview with Mother Teresa. It was one of the few she had granted to date. She resisted them mostly, probably thinking they were a waste of time when placed against the prospect of holding a dying beggar in her arms. But somehow this station secured one.

My family wasn't interested, and I didn't want to be distracted, so I went down into the basement and lugged up the old 20-inch black-and-white to my second-story bedroom. I struggled with its rabbit-ear tuning until I finally bent the telescoping arms into a sweet spot. The picture was semiclear, as long as I didn't move around. I settled in.

Some people have a talent for the economy of words. Mother Teresa had it. No statement, no answer went longer than two or three sentences. Yet their impact upon me would last for years.

The interviewer, whom I'd seen before many times, was normally the highly evolved intellectual, able to pull out the hidden side of any subject. In this piece, she seemed almost wooden— one-dimensional. With the camera angled over her shoulder to look down on Mother Teresa's tiny frame, she began. "Why, Mother Teresa? Why do you kiss the dying beggar? Why do you walk the streets searching for them?"

Without so much as a turn, she answered simply, *"Because it is Him. I am holding Him."*

"By 'him,' you mean God?" the interviewer probed.

A startled look showed on the nun's face. "Yes. Of course. God, Jesus." She shuffled on. Children ran to her. She brushed her craggy, knuckled hands against their hair, gently sweeping it off their faces. She was speaking in a language I didn't understand, but the camera captured the intent in her smile in a language I did know. Kindness. Simple touch. Attention—valuable gifts of love tumbling from her every appendage. The children clung to her, hugging her skirt as the television crew caught up.

"Mother, how do you sustain these efforts and the efforts of those who have chosen to follow you into this calling? Where does the money come from?"

She looked out at the street, at people moving like currents against one another. "People see Him here, too. They give. It is enough."

No 800 numbers keyed on the screen. No address. No solicitation.

On she went. The camera cut to a dark, barren structure where people laid on

small rugs. There were many. One severely
disfigured man lay on his pallet, his shrunken
arm gripping Mother Teresa's at the elbow.
She returned his grasp, and with her free
hand she wiped his brow, intermittently
kissing it. She was old, yet she knelt on
the bare floor beside him. She spoke to him
in soft tones that reminded me of my own
mother; sweet whispers and comforts.
His eyes struggled to stay focused on her
smiling face, but they failed and closed
with exhaustion.

There was a quiet reverence as the
interviewer continued with Mother Teresa
in the dim light of the singular window.
"Who are these people?" she asked with
the appropriate seriousness.

"Him." That's all she said, leaving
the interviewer stunned.

"But where do they come from,
Mother?"

Mother Teresa gestured with her
arm widely, vaguely, and yet there was a
specificity to it. "Out there," she said.

I found myself weeping and panicking
as I continually shifted the rabbit ears, trying
to chase away the snow from the picture. It
hindered the audio, so I was straining for her
words, already veiled by her heavy accent.

A few times I heard them sonically, but the emotional decoding took a moment. I was broken by their impact minutes after they were spoken. I stopped myself mid-blow, afraid I might miss the next. The result was a stuttering, passionate roller coaster, interrupted only by the sound of my pencil scratching on a pad. I wanted to remember her words.

At the end of the interview, I looked down at what I'd written. *All I saw was the word Him.*

How great a love. How compelling a reason to love—to live. She said, "I do because when I do—I do for Him."

Katy calls me a few days after Mother Teresa's death, and we remember her.

"You know, I think it's kind of sad that Princess Diana's death in some ways obscured the significance—the eulogistic moment—of Mother Teresa's death. I don't think she received the honor she deserved because of it."

"I disagree, Kate. I think it was exactly the way she wanted it. She'd noted the death of Diana, and I think in some ways, it released her to go herself—in the way she was accustomed to. She knew that Diana would be the focus. In truth, what

All I saw
was the word
Him.

other death could command such a response as to obscure her own?

"She slipped from us the only way she could have with the least amount of fanfare. Her death at any other time would have elicited more of the response she'd spent her life avoiding—the attention, the elevation of her simple acts of love over the reason for those simple acts."

"Hmm. Never thought of it that way." Then Katy becomes my childhood sister once again. She speaks to me the way she did under the blankets with the flashlight turned upward on her face. "Do you think they see each other up there in heaven? You know, they were friends in real life."

"I doubt it."

Disappointed, she shoots back, "Why not?"

"Because, Kate, if true beauty is visible in heaven, Mother Teresa will be a devastating bombshell, and Di will probably walk right past her."

We laugh at the innocent truth of it all. And then we fall silent, reflecting on a woman, a holy woman who spent every last bit of her existence giving, loving, touching the leper, the indigent, the mangled—all to touch Him—all to serve Him. Each stroke, each kiss carved a beauty in her, a stellar brilliance that will outlast every measurement of time as we know it.

We prepare to hang up. Kate adds, "Remember that story about Cecelia? Well, the next day I was quizzing the class on what we'd learned. I pointed to Mother Teresa's picture and called on Cecelia to tell who she was. She answered, 'Dat a saint, Ms. Becker. She's a saint.'"

Cecelia knows what she knows.

NINE
WHAT SHE KNOWS

Our eyes

finally met and we saw

    each other for

    perhaps the first time.

"*You know what this feels like*

SLOW
DRUM

don't you?"

**he
asked.**

It was not a question

in the true sense,

but more of an acknowledgment

of membership in a clandestine club.

"You tried

to tell me

once. . . ."

I wondered how long he would allow himself to be emotionally splayed before me. The tears had come, off and on, for about a half hour. The last part of it, his normally casual posture crumbled into suppressed sobs as I bent over his chair and held him from behind. Muffled, tearful breaths shook us both.

I wept as I felt his carefully maintained persona shifting before me. I wanted to hold in what he could not. I didn't need to know his vulnerability if he did not want me to.

I was not successful.

We stayed that way for a while, me whispering the assurances that were true, him desperately trying to stay the flow of emotions that moved him. The tears were not for himself, though he had good reason, but for his family. Circumstances had begun a river of events that pulled them all—wife, children, and himself—downstream to devastation. Speculation abounded, tongues were wagging, and that perhaps was the hardest part: the voices of friends and colleagues irresponsibly passing information in both smugness and mock concern. It was that cloud that began to rob this family, like thieves pillaging the smoky remains of the newly destroyed.

I wanted

to hold in

what he

could not.

*This morning
I woke with the
sun and went for a
walk on the freshly
windswept beach.
My footprints
were joined by the
light, three-pronged
patterns left
by the seagulls'
spindly talons.*

When he was finally able to sit up that evening, the gray landscape sat shrouded under the edge of advancing night. Angular shadows stretched across my back porch. A quiet hung between us that was usually awkward, but under the circumstances, it seemed moist with grace. It was the same quiet that rends the veil from the heart so that souls come straight to the surface to view one another—no pretenses, no hiding places.

Our eyes finally met and we saw each other for perhaps the first time. "You know what this feels like, don't you?" he asked. It was not a question in the true sense, but more of an acknowledgment of membership in a clandestine club. "You tried to tell me once. . . ." His voice trailed off as he stared at the candle burning on the table. Shaking his head, he continued, "This is hard. All those times I talked . . . the things I said. I didn't know."

"It is hard," was all I could offer. I knew that he finally truly understood why so many years ago I'd loved him enough to challenge his thoughtless addition to my own misery. He was part of my tears then, but not as a comforter.

We were longtime friends.
I never understood what made him harm

me for a few minutes of solicitous talk . . .
group banter . . . idle chat. Even now the
word *gossip* feels too narrow and innocuous
to define such a weapon. Harmless, dismiss-
able, overdone 40-something women on TV
sharing movie stars' movements; coffee klatch
mumbo-jumbo—those are images the word
gossip calls to mind—not this broken man in
my backyard. Not his fractured family.

The words he faced now were
perhaps the epitome of how destructive
words can be. The truth or untruth of them
had little bearing on their ability to wound
deeply. These were statements never meant
for repetition. These were statements intended not for the building of a heart but for its
harm, blemishing, sullying. In the ravaged
countenance of my friend, I could see they
had achieved their purpose.

As I studied him I remembered his
response to his own offense toward me when
I confronted him with it. He was sorry, and
our friendship recovered. Once I'd wondered
which sorrow it was: empathy or guilt. Now
as he sat across from me, his eyes reddened
with tears, I wondered no longer. He had the
haunted look of recognition. *It was the face
of understanding.*

TEN
SLOW DRUM

*The sand was more
soft than usual.
My shoes sank
deep with each
step. The wind blew
so hard that I felt
as if I could have
fallen into it, arms
outstretched, and
remained standing.
The fury of the
elements . . . it was
magnificent.*

This is contentment.

There are things in life that are known only by experience. This type of hurt was one of them. Once experienced, it becomes a gatekeeper of the tongue. The words just don't tumble out as easily. The heart stands in check, echoing the dull ache of remembrance. I knew that the next time an opportunity presented itself to him, he would be slow to speak.

"I don't understand why they have done this to us," he murmured. *"For what purpose?"*

I silently shook my head at his earnest face. What words could ever make sense of it? There were no reasons good enough to justify needlessly hurting another—certainly nothing as trite as filling the uncomfortable pauses in conversation or as selfish as discrediting someone in order to appear superior— pointing out another's failure while hiding one's own.

The circle of night began closing around us but I felt no closure inside, a feeling now familiar. There were no resolutions, no answers, only the inherent truth that even this would eventually be used for good.

I wondered if the people who spoke so irresponsibly of my friend were kissing their children good night. I wondered if they'd thought about his pain—the extra measure of it their actions brought. I wondered how long it would be before they too would be admitted to this secret society called empathy—the ability to not only recognize but actually feel another's pain. To carry it as if it were their own. To try to alleviate it before it began. To refuse to be a purveyor of it. I knew, sadly, that it would be only when they had suffered the results of someone else's careless indiscretion.

I watched his back disappear into the shadows as he walked to his car. His steps looked heavy. Their sequence sounded like a slow drum: experience, empathy, compassion . . . experience, empathy, compassion. One foot in front of the other, my friend laboriously faced the night. Although I could not go with him, the weight of his world—and the low rumble of his lesson—remained in mine.

"You've got to give,

Margaret.

Give

and it will come back to you.

ACROSS
THE
TRACKS

When you can give without feeling sad about it,

then

you've

truly given.

But not until then."

I didn't like it,

but I knew she was right.

My mom knows how to work the heart. She's positively artistic about it. When she weaves her tales of need they reek of compassion and transference: someone needs something, and you're the only one who can provide it.

Throughout my childhood, Mom maneuvered like a surgeon, knowing exactly what she wanted from me—and she always got it. This was her "gifting," and I "received" it with the appropriate results. It all started with Annie.

I never saw Annie when I was young, at least not from the front. Not that I didn't try—sometimes my neck ached from the effort. My mom saw her—a lot—mostly at Catholic church. Amidst the 600 or so people who attended Mass, that was quite a feat.

The sightings always took place as communion came to a close. With everyone's head bowed, Mom bent to whisper in my ear, discreetly motioning with her head in some general direction. "There she is—see her? Oh and look—she's so happy in those socks!" My socks. My old, favorite, navy-blue, wool knee-socks. And my favorite T-shirt, the one with colorful splatters on the front. And my favorite shorts . . . even my Halloween candy. Annie got it all because she lived "across the tracks."

We lived in a nice, quiet town on eastern Long Island. I never remembered one side of it being any worse than the other. Apparently somewhere along the route of the Long Island Railroad, the other side got rather pitiful and Annie suffered in squalor—*in deep need of all my pet possessions.*

Annie was poor. Annie's mom walked along the tracks to gather dropped coals to heat their house. Annie ate only day-old rolls for dinner. Annie was sockless and I was the one who needed to help her. And so the list went.

To be truthful, I felt sorry for Annie, but I didn't like her. The few times I thought I saw her, she seemed a bit too tall and gangly for my clothes. She didn't look like she ate my Halloween loot either—too skinny. But Mom loved her and encouraged me to do the same by being a nice girl and giving cheerfully. "Be compassionate," she would instruct. "Think about how others feel."

Annie was only one of the many needy people who peppered my childhood. My mom knew them all—globally. And she knew how to move me with their sad stories. She rehearsed them for me regularly, each tale more pained than the next. She told me to teach empathy and compassion—and sometimes just to accomplish the mundane.

Such was the case with the "starving kids in China": hungry children who apparently corresponded with my mother regularly. How I rued them bite after begrudged baked-bean bite. As my thick little legs nervously twitched on top of the phone book at the dinner table, I gagged, wishing for a measly 10-cent stamp so I could put those kids out of their misery. They could have my beans, and my peas, and my mint-jellied roast beef. I'd mail it all to them.

I remember suggesting as much to my mom. She seemed to thoughtfully consider it. But by the next dinnertime the area of need had mysteriously shifted. It seemed the Chinese were doing better, but the Jolly Green Giant who made the spinach wasn't faring too well. My obvious distaste for the fruits of his labor had hurt his feelings—and those of all of his elves.

With the Giant's visage set atop the fridge for emphasis, I had to gaze upon his agonized, work-weary smile throughout the meal. The empty frozen spinach box was a constant reminder of his long, hot days in the sun, spent on behalf of my nutritive good.

I tried to like his greens. I pretended I was Popeye. I pictured myself running faster . . . jumping higher . . . getting stronger. But it still tasted like seaweed to me. Not wanting to make anyone cry, I gave in. Mom was right: I didn't want to be the source of his sadness.

Still, our wills finally clashed forcefully. Once the veggies were going down with no protest, there was an uprising somewhere in New Mexico and the Indians stepped to the forefront. Every month, a new kitchen item arrived in the mail, avocado- or orange-colored. Saltshakers, napkin holders, sugar bowls—all sent in thanksgiving to my mother for her prayers and unselfish giving.

I thought she must be giving them a fortune because these plastic decorations looked pretty fancy. "Bra money" was what she called the cash she managed to squirrel away from the monthly household budget for the Indians. It seemed that although I wasn't wearing one yet, my bra money was wanted too. Just a nickel here, a dime there—basically a cut of my allowance.

I was a hard sell, though. Sure, the Indians were in need. But no one was starving and no one was crying, and five cents from 50 was a big chunk. As hard as she tried, Mom couldn't get my cash. My compassion had met its limits.

Then came July. I remember dragging myself into the muggy kitchen one day, my

I am loving the solitude. It's been so long since I've been alone for this long a period. I almost forgot what I do. Mostly I've been reading, walking, thinking . . .

ELEVEN
ACROSS THE TRACKS

working out and fighting endless battles of Solitaire—a game that I just can't seem to win—I keep telling myself, "Who cares?"

bare feet sticking to the hot linoleum floor. Each step sounded like fresh ink rolling off a rubber stamp. I headed straight for the freezer. I just wanted to stick my head in for a few seconds of relief.

I swung the door wide, panting. The first wave of frost rolled across my face, chilling me. I took a deep, icy breath and closed my eyes. And when I opened them, I had a vision.

Beautiful and cool, rising up from the fog like an army of shiny aluminum knights: Eskimo Pies. I blinked hard. It couldn't be. This was the "no sweets" household where ice cream was a tray of frozen orange juice cubes and where, until first grade, I thought a saltine was a cookie. *Eskimo Pies*—in *our* freezer?

I stared at the neatly aligned silver packages, stunned. They were Eskimo Pies, all right. Mom had finally broken down.

I couldn't just take one. Something as valuable and unique as that would be missed, so I had to proceed carefully, according to protocol. I called out to my mother, who was knitting in the den, no doubt listening to the whole discovery process.

"Where'd these Eskimo Pies come from, Mom?"

"I bought them." Her tone was matter-of-fact.

I took a deep,

icy breath

and closed

my eyes.

I swallowed, not allowing any excitement into my voice. "Could I have one?"

Long pause.

"Ask the Indians."

I knew it! There had to be a catch. The Indians—how did they fit in? My next response was critical, and I was tangled in tortuous riddle. I had to figure out the connection. But it was so hot . . . the pies were winking at me in the frost.

Hanging onto the door now with one hand, my head lazily loped over to one side, my body swinging, I tried to keep the whine out of my voice. "Why do I have to ask the Indians?" The condensation billowed out like smoke signals with each exhausted sway.

Long pause.

"Because that's who they belong to. And if you want one, you'll have to put 25 cents in that bank they sent us for our gifts— the one gathering dust on the counter."

Mom was going to get my money and she was going to give it to the Indians after all. It hit me that not only was she going to get my money that day, but probably every day that summer because I knew the Pies lay waiting. I'd have to have one . . . and then another. . . .

By August the little bank was too heavy to hold. On those days I was short the 25 cents I had tried reasoning with Mom about caring for her own offspring here in New York, but her response was always the same. "You've got to give, Margaret. Give and it will come back to you. When you can give without feeling sad about it, then you've truly given. *But not until then.*"

I didn't like it, but I knew she was right. By October I was putting in coins on my own, without the Pies. I felt good about helping. On some level it was like making a deposit in a Bank of Good.

By December, the Indians were out of peril and we were on to the local animal shelter . . . and so it continued with many other charitable causes until I left home. Mom still has a drawer in her hutch that holds a well-worn clothes pin. It marks the money she's set aside for someone or something in need. When I visit her, I sometimes open that drawer and the sight of the neatly folded bills causes a catch in my throat. Through a teary smile I try to picture Annie. I think I've seen her now—in the children I support and visit in Africa. I've seen her essence in their eyes and I am moved to help.

My mom gave me that present, the ability to empathize and desire to intervene. It's a beautiful, humbling gift—the honor of helping. More precious than Eskimo Pies, it turns out.

You must wrestle with it,

Margaret.

Let no one

assist or relieve you.

This is for your bettermen

and perhaps,

WITH

if your dreams align with God's,

it

is

the

beginning

of your artistic journey.

Try to see the art in the struggle.

Pray that God gives you

the strength and the wisdom to love it . . .

NEW EYES

I sit in the outer office, nervously jiggling my leg. Ripples skitter down the side of my pink wool skirt. Cream silk shirt, pumps, lipstick: I am in my best.

I've never done anything like this before. I've thought about it, but just didn't know whom to go to. But Scott vouched for this guy, claimed he was the real deal and had all sorts of insights. If Scott—the ultimate in complicated—could benefit, then surely I will, too.

"Come in, Margaret." He stands long and dark in the doorway. Definitely a professor, hair greased back and wearing a 20-year-old brown-tweed suit jacket. His steps are intentional, slow, as if thoughts proceed from each gentle placement. "Please, sit down." He motions, his long bony fingers raking the air toward a well-worn green Naugahyde chair with brass tacks outlining the frame.

His office is dark, attic-like. It has the feeling of dust, though none is visible. Books spill from every corner: in piles, on shelves, stacked on top of cardboard boxes. *At least he's learned,* I think hopefully, afraid of yet another disappointment.

As he settles himself into a creaky wooden chair from the forties, I survey the books, trying to read the titles still legible on the frayed bindings—nothing I recognize. I watch him clear his desk. His hair is still jet black, unruly strands falling forward as he organizes a stack of papers. I make a wish as he sweeps it back, that he is indeed all that Scott said. I've done everything I know how to do, and still I am in this state.

My life has felt like it had one foot nailed to the floor for several years now. Wearing a circle into the ground around me in so many different ways, I've almost become convinced that this was my final position: miserable.

It was a jumble of frustrating events, from the large to the small, all sprouting and flourishing at once. I couldn't find a job with opportunity, although I was overqualified for many that I'd interviewed for. I couldn't free myself from this dream of writing and performing, although there were no opportunities appearing. Relationships around me were in turmoil. My car was falling apart, a metaphor of my life. No money, no prospects, no escape hatch. *I was in turmoil with no way out.*

I couldn't bring about my own movement in this bottomless sea of inertia. It moved me, though, to the brink of despair on more than one occasion. I'd finally concluded that real life wasn't supposed to be so frustrating, so constricting—so devoid of hope.

I'd been to the pastor. I'd fasted and prayed myself down to 100 pounds. I'd been to all the self-help seminars, read all the "how to get a job" books. Nothing changed. It just seemed that the frame of my life, like some sand castle by the sea in rising tide, was overrun with setback after setback until there was only a smooth pit of swimming sand swallowing me up.

My best friend, Scott, had been holding my hand through this. "It'll pass, Mag," he'd say with each new event. "I know that you'll get some direction soon," he said at the end of each prayer. With his brow prematurely creased on my behalf, he deluged me with sermons, tapes, books—whatever he could find to help dig me out. But even he was baffled.

In a last-ditch effort, he talked me into seeing Dr. Breene, a teacher from his college. Warning me not to pay too much attention to appearances, he assured me that the man had insight.

I was tired of waking up in tears without hope. The linoleum floor in my bedroom was too familiar to me, from all

the prostrate moanings sent heaven's way.
Although I didn't feel like pouring out my
soul to a stranger, it was for only this one
time and maybe just telling it from beginning
to end would make me feel better. So I agreed.

And here we are now, in the powdery
afternoon light: Dr. Breene and I, sitting in
silence in his closet-office at the college.
He starts. "So, why are you here?" He flips
a pencil over and over between his thumb
and his forefinger.

The simple question punctures me.
This dam of emotions has more force than I
had recognized. I don't want to break. I begin
having second thoughts. "Well, I don't know
where to start, actually." I consider faking
the whole thing—just getting out of there—
but decide against it. I begin the saga.

"I am at a dead stop in my life.
I can't seem to get a foothold one way or
another. I'm a burden to my parents because
I can't get a job that will allow me to move
out. There are many things I know I can do
well, but the opportunities are not there. I'm
an artist of sorts, and of course my dream is
to express my art. But that seems impossible
now. And yet it haunts me, like something
you have in your memory that you wish you
could change."

It hurts to speak so plainly. My knees begin shaking as if I am too cold, but I can feel the moisture of heat on my back. I continue, "I'm willing to let it go. In fact I pray for it to go, but it doesn't. And when I try to do other things—anything that might become a career—the doors slam shut in my face.

"I feel hopeless. Some days I don't want to face it anymore. This has been going on for years now, and I don't know what to do. Usually, I'm very resourceful, I can fix just about anything, but I've done all I know how to do and I can't stop this circle."

I let out a shaky sigh, noticing that I've moved forward in my seat quite a distance. I slowly lean back into a proper right angle. "That's it, Dr. Breene. Does any of this make sense to you?" I feel like a child asking things of Santa Claus, not sure if he's the right guy for the job, but hoping anyway. "Can you help me find something to hold onto in this—a hidden thread that I can pull to begin unraveling this net?"

He considers all I've told him, hands clasped and set like a tepee before the door of his mouth. Finally he speaks. "You say you've done everything that you know how to do?" he asks, summarizing.

A glimpse of hope. Maybe he will help. "Yes. Everything."

"And all your strengths have been ineffectual?"

He's leading me. . . . "Yes. All my strengths amounted to nothing."

"Hmm."

"Hmm"? Please, God, let him say more than "Hmm."

"First off, Margaret, let me say that I think that you are right where you should be right now. You are in what I would call God's greenhouse. What I mean is that a greenhouse is an environment where growth is accelerated. It's not comfortable in there. Hot, wet, a lot of pruning—not a particularly clean environment, either—but the best for growth. That's where I think you are."

He speaks with a calm. I carefully gather his words like tiny white stones that will eventually form a path leading me out.

Pausing, he swings slightly in his chair, considers life on the other side of the window. "And second, I tell you honestly, I'm frightened."

He's frightened?

"I'm frightened that I may interfere with what is obviously a sacred surgery taking place in your life right now." He moves his body back to the edge of his desk so that we face one another. He looks into my eyes without familiarity, but with clarity and purpose. "I am only a man, Margaret. My hands are of flesh, and although there are things I could probably tell you, do for you, to ease this course, I dare not because I believe this struggle is for your strengthening. And if I begin cutting the bonds, loosening the cords, you will emerge weaker for it.

"Perhaps it's a little like nature, the way a moth larvae changes into a butterfly. It is the struggle against the cocoon that sends blood into its wings so they will be strong enough to navigate the wind. Without that struggle, the wings would come out, but they would be deformed where it matters the most—inside. *Pretty, but no strength.*"

He leans in slightly for emphasis. "So you must wrestle with it, Margaret. Let no one assist or relieve you. This is for your betterment and perhaps, if your dreams align with God's, it is the beginning of your artistic journey. Try to see the art in the struggle. Pray that God gives you the strength and the wisdom to love it, because it is His great love for you that allows it. You must be prepared."

My leg ceases moving. I have a hot, puffy cloud in my throat. I don't want to cry in front of Dr. Breene, but two tears escape me. *What an odd way to look at pain and despair.*

He sits politely across from me, requiring nothing.

I am being prepared . . . hope. I feel like I am liquid, liquid with direction. I am no longer held down. My foot is freed. I have escaped in the most unusual way, through the most unexpected means. The knowledge is cathartic.

I look around his office again as he stares at the blotter. He allows the quiet to separate him from his words. He wants no recognition, no legacy for my emancipation. It is a kind gesture that allows me to fill every nook and cranny of my mind with the balm of his wisdom.

I close my eyes and mentally take my two hands, knitting them together, fingers inward, in the middle of my chest. In my mind, I peel back, with all the strength I can muster, what is left of my armor, my shielding. I expose the raw flesh of my beating heart. *If this is surgery, then let us be done with it,* I pray. *Let us get every last bit of shadow, every speck of fear. And these strengths— break them into bits. They are of no use to me, as I have seen.*

These moments, although staggering in their beauty and eccentricity, cannot be hoarded. They are for the day, for the moment, for this moment of my life. Like manna, if held a day too long, they lose their redemptive character, their ability to nourish and heal.

I stand to leave, and though I am heavy with emotion, I feel unbearably light, like there is no gravity. I know there is more struggle ahead, more surgical steel, but I have hope for the healing, vision for recovery.

I leave Dr. Breene's office with that one thread in my hand, the key to it all. I watch with new eyes as the mystery begins to unravel.

He bends his neck back
with delight,

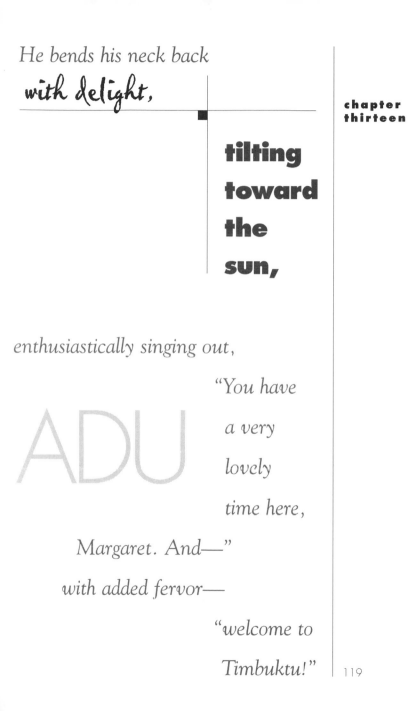

**tilting
toward
the
sun,**

enthusiastically singing out,

ADU

"You have
a very
lovely
time here,
Margaret. And—"
with added fervor—
"welcome to
Timbuktu!"

"**M**y name is Ahh-doo . . . Ahh-doo, madam, and what is yours?" A long, spindly, chocolate arm is firmly raised above the dusty throng of children amassed in a circle around me.

"Madam! Madam! What is your name?" the voice connected to the arm sings out. The arm wavers from the force of the crowd shifting back and forth. It is 120 degrees in the shade, I am in the Sahara desert in a town I've often joked about visiting— Timbuktu, Africa. I am hotter than I ever imagined anyone could be. Every breath feels like a dusty brown cotton ball in my throat. Everywhere I look, I see children running to meet me and the rest of our party. The voice chimes out again, almost in song; the lovely English spoken with a tinge of French accent adds to the surreal film that layers my senses. "Madam, my name is Adu!"

I reach out to the hand and firmly shake it as the force of the crowd propels me along with it. I feel as if I'm in a stupor, drunk with heat. The hand pulls itself toward me and the crowd parts a little. Emerging is a beautiful young African boy dressed in a deep-indigo serape, with a matching blue turban. His smile is broad. He gently holds onto me a little longer as he sidles up, walking elbow to elbow, as if we are old friends discussing serious matters.

"And your name, madam?" he asks much more softly now, with the appropriate cock of the head.

I have no strength. To resist is futile, although I am sure this will all lead somehow to exchange of money and goods. "Margaret," I answer in a collapsed breath.

"Aaahh. . . . Margaret, is it?" he asks, like a wise old man gently prodding me to reconsider the validity of something I've just spoken. I am amused, but I have no strength to smile. The hotel is within sight, and even though it looks like an East L.A. car junkyard from a distance, I have hope.

"Margaret, is this your first time to Timbuktu?" Adu lilts on, voice completely distinctive against the murmur of the other childlike exchanges going on around us. The question seems absurd. I'm wiping my brow, massaging the heat headache from my temples. We are in the middle of the desert. There are no roads, a few straw huts, no trees.

"Yes," I answer, exhausted and marveling at his interviewing techniques. Quite tenacious, he is. I steal a quick glimpse of him. He has regal features, long and aquiline. I learn later that he is a Turag, a member of an ancient nomadic tribe that has traversed the desert trade routes of Northern Africa for centuries. It is a stunning race, known not only for its unique beauty but also its traditional dress: indigo clothing.

"You will find it lovely! There are many things to see." Adu gestures toward the rest of the desert. I see nothing but camels, sand, and perhaps a mirage of a tall glass of ice water.

We walk farther, the throng still equally distributed around us like a human tutu. Adu's hands are entwined behind his back and his head hangs slightly. When he is listening to my words, he assumes the posture of a sage. I decide to confront the inevitable right away. I'm too depleted for niceties. "Adu, I am not going to buy anything from you. I did not bring money and I don't want any souvenirs." I've taken a chance and perhaps insulted him, but I don't want him to waste his time on me. I know that there are other marks in the crowd who do want something of Timbuktu to take home.

His is not the only arm that reaches out to me. It kills me to deny any of them, but to give to one and not all is more painful still. We are here with World Vision in an effort to empower this group of people to help themselves without upsetting the equilibrium of their culture by inserting ourselves. After visiting many areas of need much like this one, I see the wisdom in the slow process of a culture righting itself by its own power—instead of remaining in the "quick fix" cycle of western dependency.

Our hope is to identify what impedes them from being self-sufficient, and to provide them with the knowledge and tools to overcome. We don't want to leave any impression at all, save the spirit of our help: the command to love our brother as ourselves. It seems a much more lasting answer to this problem, even though for now, in the midst of the beggars and children, it feels uncaring.

I take comfort for Adu, knowing we are here to bring much more than a couple of dollars, to many more than those who know how to ask. If we succeed at our mission in the next few days, we will bring him and his companions more than he could dream of. Adu will have to wait, but it will go well for him shortly.

Adu is resilient. He is not slighted by my remark, but in fact uses it as a tool to overcome my resistance. Out from his draping sleeve comes a meticulously handcrafted, silver, single-blade pocket knife in a tooled black leather sheath. The pitch begins, like a song, a siren's call. "Margaret, do you not want a lovely handcrafted souvenir to show your friends at home? It is fine, is it not?" It is indeed as it sits in his tiny palm. "Only 20 American dollars. I would be happy to have American dollars!"

Now the pitch takes an unexpected turn, his tone becomes *sotto voce*, decrescendo in small increments. It causes me to bend nearer to hear him. "Oh . . . and you will enjoy this for . . . to come. . . . You must have. . . ."

I can't hear him any longer, though I know he's talking. Somehow I feel he is my friend and I address him finally as such at the gate of my hotel. "Adu, I'm not buying but some in our party will. Work on some others, you'll be better off."

The crowd begins to loosen and he stands amidst them like a tiny ambassador fitly adorned. As he thrusts his hands out to the sides and raises them to his shoulders, it seems as if he holds all of Timbuktu in his grasp and offers it to me generously in his final statement. Loudly he exclaims, "Well, all right then, Margaret." He bends his neck back with delight, tilting toward the sun,

It's getting late now. The ocean has become invisible. Around the house candles are burning.

MARGARET
BECKER

I hear a steady stream of rainwater splattering down onto the wooden deck. As the blackness settles around me, I wonder if there is anything in life that can be truly captured.

enthusiastically singing out, "You have a very lovely time here, Margaret. And—" with added fervor— "welcome to Timbuktu!"

The memory of it trails behind him as he turns and skips into the desert, making his way across it toward something that looks like an anthill from where I stand. The other children filter after him, giggling and running, also finished with me.

I watch until Adu is a blue dot on a light tan canvas, a rocket with a tumble of children as his aura. I turn back to the hotel, a sand-colored structure built on sand in the middle of sand that makes me want to cough. I am sure there is sand in my throat. I see two emaciated goats on the left and hear a sound which will become familiar to me by the end of my visit. It is a death knell of sorts: the shuffle of well-worn sandals in sand. It is the way these people move about. Only the children actually have the energy to lift their feet. The rest of the population conserves what precious strength is granted them by moving in tiny increments with exacting slowness. Fast is not a word often associated with Timbuktu. *I see why.*

I am here to film a 30-hour Famine video with World Vision. I've seen firsthand in many places the good that is done by the

From the profound to the mundane, like mercury in a fist, they endlessly slip and meld, cleaving to new surfaces for split moments . . .

THIRTEEN
ADU

enchanting new hearts. And this clarity of thought, this visual feast of grey hues, will escape me too; as did the frogs and baubles before them.

voluntary fast they call the "famine," and I am committed to sing its praises. I remind myself of that commitment when we stand at the front desk and hear the truth about Timbuktu first-class accommodations: there is no electricity, only a diesel generator that is turned on daily from two to four in the afternoon and from nine at night to six in the morning. That means no light, no air conditioning, no nothing. Adu's words of welcome ring in my ears. I chuckle.

The next morning, exhausted from the night's activities—chasing ten-inch lizards from my cement room, and contorting my cot to the mockery of an air conditioner hung loosely in the wall—I wake to the sensation of someone laying a dry, hot blanket over my entire body. I am suffocating. In my panting I hear roosters crowing. On some level my brain coalesces the scene and recognizes it as the beginnings of dementia.

I force my eyes open in protest to a pitch-black room. Something is missing in the dead silence. As the dry heat fills my lungs it dawns on me: the electricity has gone off. I shine my penlight on my travel clock. Only 4:30 A.M. *I thought the air*—hot breath, in truth—*was on until 6 A.M.!*

Searching for my sandals and praying

to avoid lizard skin, I sit on the edge of the bed. The situation begins revealing itself, a tangle of impossible knots. We are shooting film today and I have to shower, dry my hair, put on camera makeup accurately, and learn new lines—all without the benefit of electricity in the impenetrable darkness. Thus the day begins. I say a simple prayer. "You know what we must do, Lord. I can't do it without proper tools. *Please work it out.*"

How surprised I am when we are en route, just over an hour later, to a building across town with a working outlet. I am surprised not only by the resourcefulness managed during the whole ordeal, but by Adu, who is holding court outside the main gate already at this early hour. Dressed in his serape, playing some sort of tag with three other children, he is even more rejuvenated by the relative cool—only 90 degrees at this hour. "Margaret! Good morning! Good morning, Marc!" he adds to my companion. Running to us, he inquires, "Where are you going?"

"I'm going to the blue hotel to get some electricity."

"I see." He gently reaches for my arm and slips a silver bracelet on my wrist. He has thought some from the day before, tailored his pitch to me. The sing-songy offer begins.

"Yes, this is beautiful—no? Lovely for a lady. You will wear it and remember Timbuktu, Margaret. You must have it. . . ."

I take it off and place it back in his hand, and the tapering starts. "Oh, but you know you should have this. It is so very. . . ."

I can't make out the words. I look him in the eye. "Sorry, Adu. I'm not buying. I'm really not, my friend."

Unruffled by my resistance, his voice becomes full once again. "Okay, then. Goodbye until later!"

I know there will surely be more "later."

That morning, we are shuttled about in an old, dilapidated Peugeot with Robert, the local missionary and a Crocodile Dundee look-alike, at the wheel. He navigates like a pro, without the help of any signs or markers. With no air conditioning in the car, even a dusty movement-induced breeze of heat seems more bearable than the still. I reach to put down my window. No handle. I look up. Robert, all knowing, is holding the lone handle. "Been here 15 years with my family. This is the best vehicle we've had, but we still have to share the crank."

In transportation held together by spit and bungee cords, we slide along the desert floor from location to location, all

before 11 A.M., at which point the heat
brings waves of dizziness. All the locals
withdraw into cover, even if it is only the
shade offered by a leafless bush.

I see Adu hovering nearby throughout
the day, working our crowd and commanding
an audience. He is my "fanner" for part of
the afternoon video shoot, using a big green
leaf to cool me between takes. We speak of
camels, commerce, and his family. During
a particularly long lapse he points across the
shimmering valley to a straw igloo. "You see
that? There, Margaret. You see?"

"Yes, Adu. What is it?"

"It is my house. You must come today
for afternoon tea—yes? Come and visit."

It looks about a mile away, and
although the idea of tea in the Sahara
intrigues me, we are leaving shortly and
we are not finished. "Adu, I'm afraid I must
decline. We are leaving soon. My apologies."

"Next time, then," he says, cupping
my elbow. He puts down his green leaf in
order to chase away some other children.
As he runs I notice a patch of fabric peeking
out from the opening of his blue robe. It
looks like white fabric with little red hearts,
but I'm sure I must be mistaken. We are in
the middle of nowhere.

Time speeds up as our departure draws near. Adu and a few chosen cohorts help us load back into the Peugeot. The camera crew, Marc, and I jam in. The parting comes swiftly as Adu places a trinket in the hands of Dan the cameraperson. "Only two American dollars, Dan. This is handcrafted. You should have it now because—"

"No thanks, Adu. Thanks for all your help," Dan responds.

"Goodbye, Margaret! Goodbye, Marc. We will see you again!" he proclaims after us, the tireless emissary once again. "Tell Michael Jackson to visit." We have no idea how he knows of Michael Jackson.

Relieved to be only four hours away from a cold shower, we all relax. With our heads tilted back in the hot breeze, the wind doesn't even nudge our matted hair. We've not even left and we begin to relive it all.

"Man. That Adu. What a salesman, huh?" Dan starts.

"Yeah. He was good, but I didn't buy anything." I notice that Marc has different clothes on, almost dress clothes. "Hey, Marc, did you change? Where are those old sneakers you've been wearing?"

"Umm . . . I left them."

"Left them? Where? At the hotel? Maybe we should go back—"

"No. I left them on purpose. With Adu."

"Adu? You gave Adu your shoes?" Paul, the producer, laughs.

"Yeah, and a few other things I didn't need."

White and red fabric flashes in my mind. "Would that include underthings, Marc?" I inquire.

"Oh. Yeah. Guess you saw my Valentine's boxers. Hope my wife doesn't mind. Adu put them on right in front of me. You would have thought I gave him a camel or something."

"He got a few T-shirts off me, too. Said they were for his friends," Paul admits.

"It's funny, though," I muse, "none of us even bought his stuff."

We consider this when Dan reaches into his pocket and pulls out the first item presented for sale—the silver knife in the sheath. Much laughter follows. "How much you pay for that, Dan?" Paul asks.

He hesitates, then stammers, "You know . . . he did help me carry my gear, and turned out to be a great conversationalist. . . . I gave him 20 dollars. He deserved it."

He did deserve it. That and so much more.

I picture Adu the next time the twin-engine plane brings a load of hot tourists. I see him confident in his Valentine boxers and oversized Nikes, charming the lot. I am happy that my friends were softer than I was, and rewarded his ingenue. I have no regret, though. He and I understood each other from the first, and forged a relationship despite the financial arrangement. I think that is a credit to us both. And within a few months, Adu and his friends will begin to feel the impact brought by the donations of sponsors. I am confident that when I return, he will be mayor.

I watch his straw city fade from sight and review his graciousness. I am enchanted. Ambassador Adu has left with me "something" of Timbuktu after all. The best thing, even: himself.

WHISTLING IN THE DARK

I giggle.

My tomboy sister is

in a ponytail wig.

She shoots me a sharp look
in the mirror,

but

she's

not

mad.

Is this what happens

when you become

a "teenager"?

Karen Curka looks like a mannequin with catlike, black tapered lines around her eyes.

She works them in lazy, trained sweeps, like Bette Davis, as she fusses over my sister Kate.

We are up in Karen's bedroom. She's got Kate seated in front of her at the pink vanity table. I'm sitting on the floor trying to be still, lucky to be here; they usually ditch me halfway through the woods.

"This is what's cool, Katy. See this?" Karen says as she pulls my sister's shoulder-length hair into a tight, high ponytail. It lasts for a second before strands slip free.

"I think my hair's too short."

Karen ponders the problem. "I know! Let's try this!" She reaches into her own hair and pulls her ponytail right off, like a magic trick. Karen Curka wears a wig, only it's not a wig because it's just one long piece, not a whole head of hair like my Aunt Maureen. I stare at her teeth, wondering if they come off, too, like my Aunt's.

"Let's see if this is your shade." She speaks in wispy breaths like a hairdresser and holds up the tail to Katy's head. "It'll do." Skillfully, she begins inserting bobby pins that seem to disappear into Kate's scalp.

I giggle. My tomboy sister is in a ponytail wig. She shoots me a sharp look in the mirror, but she's not mad.

Is this what happens when you become a "teenager"? I consider my teenaged brother, clomping through the house. He doesn't talk to any of us anymore—just goes straight to his room, closes the door, and turns on the stereo really loud. That's how boys do it, I guess. I guess girls get wigs.

Next Karen paints my sister's eyelids with a tiny brush. It tickles Katy and she blinks, making the lines go crooked. Then Karen's leading Kate across the floor, showing her how to move her hips like the girls on *American Bandstand*. Katy is stiff and I wonder if it's because I'm here. I haven't been invited before. I wonder if they do this all the time.

Before the night is through, Katy gets the works: hair, makeup, nails, dancing. I say next to nothing. Fascinated and squeamish, I wonder if I'm going to like it when it all happens to me.

It's dark when we make our way home. All the lines and colors long washed off her face for fear of discovery, Katy carries the wig in her hand. It looks like a ferret. The plan is to bring it to Catholic school tomorrow in a bag and try to attach it in

I try to

be brave,

but I can't.

the bathroom. I'm privy to the deception and I feel tingly, like a spy.

Mrs. Paray's woods separate our houses. It's only a quarter of an acre, but it feels like a vast jungle to me. I'm afraid as we enter the dense overgrowth but don't say so immediately in case anyone evil is within earshot. I don't want enemies to know how easily they could capture me in this shaky state. I try to be brave, but I can't. "You scared, Kate?" I whisper. I'm walking softly like the Indians do.

"A little," she whispers back, eyes darting all around the woods.

"Nothing'll happen to us . . . right?" I can tell she's scared because I am almost running to keep pace with her.

She slows down suddenly and answers in full voice, as if to announce, "You know what you do when you're scared?"

I'm relieved. "What?" I imitate her tone, following her lead.

 she states, loud and matter-of-fact. Staring straight ahead she adds, "Let's just whistle together." Our strides become more leisurely and I calm. I'm not so good at whistling—mine produces more spit than sound—but Katy's loud enough for the both of us.

*I close my eyes
tightly and press
the already fading
memories into my
mind. I pray that
they find their
way to my soul, to
the place where
the most deserving
memories catalog
themselves by
fragrance. Their
breath eludes me,
but their fragrance
remains.*

When we're at the gate to our yard, she smacks my arm lightly and makes a break for the light at the back door. The suddenness of it makes me scream involuntarily as I tear after her. She was scared the whole time, even during the whistle.

We're laughing loudly as we wipe our feet. "Scared ya, didn't I?" she says with a mock taunt between rushed breaths.

"No! No, you didn't!" It's my natural programmed response to any question that comes dressed up in that tone.

She puts her hand on my head as we walk in. She knows the truth.

The tiny twelve-seater airplane affords me only a small aperture to the dark sky outside. Katy is in the seat next to me and we're out of breath once again. Delayed connections from our respective cities left us heaving luggage over shoulders, winding through tendrils of people. I'm used to this but I was worried for her. People were already boarding when I finally saw her reddened face appear at the end of the hallway. *I was relieved, knowing that we would go together.*

"Want something to drink?" I offer, once we're comfortable.

Kate looks up and down the tiny aisle. "This plane is too small to serve, isn't it?"

"No, they'll serve in a moment.
I am dying of thirst." I glance around, too,
for the flight attendant. "Sorry about the
tight connection. What an ordeal, huh?"

"Wasn't your fault. Hate this airline.
Don't fly this one, Margaret—too many
crashes."

"I know. I hate it, too." We sit back
and let out long breaths in stereo; a mutual
habit I've never noticed before. We get our
drinks and pass on the nuts.

"You ready for this?" I ask her. Her
face in the tight beam of the overhead light
reminds me of an orange-plastic study lamp
we had on our bedroom desk. She almost
convinced me once that it was made of
human skin.

She looks at the separation between
the two seats in front of us, then to me.

"No. Not really." Another sip. "You?"

"As much as I can be," I say, but
when it reaches her, I'm not sure if it's true.
We're going to face a crisis of sorts. It stands
much bigger than either of us. I don't know
whether to address it further, for fear some
entity will overhear and know how easily we
can be mowed down. I don't want to clothe
my questions in words; as if words would bind
the worst to us, making us responsible to it.

Instead, I identify my fears as a feeling whose shape I know—black branches knit like a net, looming against the night sky. We walk along under it softly, like the Indians did.

I sense her fear. The words get caught in the middle of my tongue, but with resolve and a bit of childlike awkwardness I can't disguise, I whisper to my sister, "You scared?"

She swallows. "A little."

We can't whistle in here. I reach out and place my hand on her leg just above her knee, giving it a squeeze. Even through her jeans, I recognize its familiar form and visualize it in miniature; just the same from a thousand summer days, sharp and muscled. Strong. I see it flying around the bases at softball games and straining on the pedals of a big blue bike. I believe in its strength, and although my own grew to be much more compact, I'm thinking that together we might have a chance.

"At least we're together," she says.

"I know, Kate." I turn to her, making sure she can see both my eyes. *"I'm glad you're here."*

She places her hand on top of mine and its warmth settles me. We're comfortable like that for a few moments, still in the shad-

ows, knowing there are no easy escapes.

"Guess we just have to go through,"
I announce, full-voiced, with no emotion at all.

She follows, glancing around the
plane, making one eye wider than the other,
the way Sherlock Holmes used to—a secret
spy signal.

Katy clears her throat and says,
"Guess so." She says it deliberately, with
defiant authority, to all who will hear.

She releases my hand and I change
my mind about the nuts. We move on to talk
about our friends and families. All the while,
I'm staring straight ahead in my heart, looking for the back-door light so I can slap her
arm and race her to its edge.

FOURTEEN
*WHISTLING
IN THE DARK*

As I watched him,

my mind slipped

back through the years.

I remembered curling up

in the warmth of his lap

where I would hear

I remembered his strong hands playfu

I remembered

his inexhaustible patience

NEW

magnificent stories of kings and princesses

from far-off places.

hisking me off my feet into his safe embrace.

with my endless questions . . .

GROUND

I remember how thick the air felt in my room when I awoke that morning. The month of July in this bedroom was always sticky. For a moment I lay and adjusted to the sounds of the creek, the birds, the cicadas. I thought about how different these sounds were from what I was used to—car horns and the dull whine of rubber on pavement.

At my house in Tennessee, the sounds were of struggle: people rushing from here to there in pursuit of the ever elusive dollar; people hurrying anywhere for a few precious moments of peace. They were sounds of a journey in heated progression.

Here at my parents' retirement home, the sounds were of arrival; of a journey well taken. There were no neighbors shouting to children, no traffic noise at 8:30 A.M., just the occasional pickup truck on its way to the local store for a paper. I guess that's why the clanking I heard caught my ear. *That's strange*, I thought, glancing at the clock. *It's only nine. What is that?* I listened for a moment. It was a methodical sound whose rhythm I soon recognized. I brushed my curtains aside to see my father.

His reddened face beaded with perspiration, his expression taut with determination, he stood in the middle of the yard pushing a rusty hoe deep into the hard ground. Ten feet around him, in a perfect square, lay dark red, freshly overturned topsoil. It took me a moment to realize what he was doing. The year had been a dry one and the grass, once a carpet of green, now receded into small, disconnected patches of brown stubble. It was not the first time I had seen him turn over topsoil before planting new seed.

He was a diligent worker and I was evidence of it. He had taken a hoe to my life on many occasions, breaking up the fallow ground of my heart, assessing my needs and planting seeds of truth along the way. When I was overwhelmed, he reminded me of my strength. When I was wrong, his correction came swiftly and ended with a hug of assurance: it was forgotten. When I needed his advice, he gave it with respect and caution. He even allowed me a few "weeds" along the way to show me the cost of freedom and the importance of choosing wisely.

As I watched him, my mind slipped back through the years. I remembered curling up in the warmth of his lap where I would hear magnificent stories of kings and princesses from far-off places. I remembered his strong hands playfully whisking me off my feet into

The fire is snapping; the air smells like a potpourri of burning wood, vanilla, cinnamon, and the sea. These days are better than I ever could have imagined. I am so thankful to be alive. . . so thankful to be so intricately cared for.

his safe embrace. I remembered his inexhaustible patience with my endless questions . . . the shadow of his body on the dining room table as he checked the answers to my homework . . . the cool of the evening air fresh on his hand as he lay it on my fevered brow . . . the gentleness of his step at the yearly father-daughter square dance. I had so many wonderful memories.

As I looked at him that sticky summer morning, it was as if I saw him for the first time: This was my father, an honest man, a kind man, a man who had spent his entire life giving to others.

The tears that brimmed my eyes were a surprise. I wondered what memory had passed my mind and pierced my heart unbeknownst to me. Surely these were all happy memories, nothing to cry over. Nothing that would justify the gnawing in the pit of my stomach.

Looking around my room, my eyes resting on nothing, I searched myself for an answer. Seconds later I looked back out at my father. The warm explosion in my chest felt so unexpected yet so familiar. With stinging clarity the truth revealed itself: How many Saturday mornings had I heard these very same sounds—the dull thud of a shovel, the whir of the lawn mower, the

How many
times had I
told him that
I love him?

terse clipping of the shears—how many times had I rolled over for another half hour of sleep? How many late Sunday afternoons had I watched my father stiffly lower himself onto the couch, more exhausted from the weekend's chores than he ever was from his normal eight-to-seven workday?

How many times had I told him that I love him? How many times had I assured him that he was an excellent father, generous in the needful things like love and attention—and time? How many opportunities had I let slip by to show him, the way he showed me every day of his life, that I cared?

In that moment I understood the broad scope of love that is the backbone of fatherhood: the constant unnoticeables, the many details that are silently taken care of. I thought about how God, in His fatherly provision, had taken such care in this detail for me—providing this man. Few things have ever made me as thankful as the simple act of breathing did in that moment. *I was here, he was here—there was still time.*

Hurriedly I slipped out of bed. I put on shorts and sneakers and wiped the tears from my chin. I bowed my head for just a

moment. "Thank You, Lord, for the wonderful man You have given me for a father."

I'll never forget the look on his face when I came around the corner with the metal rake in hand.

"What are you doing up so early, Maggie?" he asked.

"I came out to help you, Dad."

He smiled warmly, with an expression I'd seen only a few times over the years—the kind that hears the unspoken regrets, senses the rawness of the moment, and allows it to pass graciously—the kind that only someone with a parental bond can give. We began to turn over new ground, and with each pull of the ancient rake, I felt a joy and excitement that only comes from reconciling a long overdue debt of love.

Many nights I've laid awake,
wondering

what could be so strong,

so overwhelming

that it could overshadow God's

act of love toward us —

His sacrifice

made in the form of a man.

What materials is that fence made of?

What stones

form that wall?

STONES

I guess I didn't get it. Most times there are dangling ends somewhere that you can connect to make some sort of linear sense of situations. But in this there were no matches that I could see.

This was about love, was it not?

Mercy, the gift unearned—and forgiveness, absolute and complete. That's why people bothered with faith. That's what drew people to Jesus. That's what brought me to this place. Then why these wild and loose ends and edges?

"They want to meet with us tonight," Cindy announced.

"I can't believe they said those things!"

My roommates chattered at one another over my head at Shoney's. I was buried in my salad. Although these women were a scant few years my senior, they were older "in the Lord," which I thought meant "wiser" than I.

Noting my silence, they stopped, considering their words more carefully. I wasn't looking, but I am sure that cautionary glances were exchanged. Without a word, some neo-parental decision was made and Cindy stepped up to the plate.

"You see, Mag, sometimes there are these misunderstandings between brothers and sisters and . . . well, sometimes words that shouldn't be spoken are spoken, and—uh. . . ." She searched Jan's face for help.

Jan continued, "People have differences. We believe the same, but—"

"Sounds like real life to me," I mumbled through my chickpeas.

I saw alarm on their faces. My first few months in this heightened state of relationship with Jesus were not supposed to remind me of "real life." They were supposed to be some netherworld that kept me mesmerized and fooled into keeping a commitment long enough to believe it for real.

"It's not what you think, Margaret. This is just a misunderstanding among family, so to speak. There is no malicious intent," Cindy offered.

I took a sip of Coke. "Yeah, I understand what you're both saying. It's all right. It's not the first time this has happened to me, okay? It's the same everywhere. People don't like other people for one reason or another and they do things to tear them down. That's essentially what this is." Shrugging, I added, "Just so happens that they are doing it over 'Christian' things."

Worried glances flew around the table. Forks were placed neatly at the side of

plates and throats cleared. I got the talk—
the one about how Christians are different
and disagreements between them are essentially exempt of base motivations. Most hurtful
words are for our own good and we are sharpened by them. Many of them are God-inspired
for our growth, and that was why this gossip
about the spiritual state of our household was
different from the gossip I heard last semester
about how I was "rude and stupid" because

I was a _____ Yankee.

It felt the same to me. And I didn't
understand why the Baptist boys were criti-
cizing us for going to a nondenominational
church. We all believed in Jesus—right?
We all believed in His words—right? Then
what was the difference? My roommates
tried to explain it several times more,
but it didn't make sense.

Still doesn't.

Many nights I've laid awake, wondering what could be so strong, so overwhelming
that it could overshadow God's act of love
toward us—His sacrifice made in the form of
a man. What can dwarf that act and erect so
great a barrier that people who essentially
claim to share the same lifeblood are at bitter
odds with one another? What materials is
that fence made of? What stones form that

wall? What mortar can withstand the heat of His love and make enemies of friends?

When I think of the lines drawn between "us" and "them," I stagger. They are lines of separation that celebrate nuance and preference, and raise them up as singularly correct—absolute. In reality these are choices we make for ourselves, our own comfort— and we force them like straitjackets on one another, all in the name of God. It's frightening, or at the very least, codependent.

There is something very disturbing about the vehemence that rises up in us all when we believe our very center of existence has been offended. That bile is almost uncontrolled; believing we're righteous, we use it as a license to wound, a carte blanche for cruelty. I've watched that bile appear over small things like differences over the expressions of worship, and bigger, more hideous things like church affiliation.

Criticisms, corrections, lines, even attacks—all for the sake of the "acceptable" order of things. Yet Jesus Himself drew the greatest line when He dragged His forefinger in the dust. Kneeling before a prostitute He challenged the "holy" men of that day who brought her forward to be stoned. "He who is without sin—cast the first stone."

I have no

strength to

carry stones.

I've often wondered if He connected line to line, forming words, titles recognizable only to the individual. *Adulterer*. One man leaves. *Thief*. Another stone drops. *Murderer*. Yet another. *Liar. Heretic. Hypocrite*. No one remains. I'm sure that these failings were not hidden from Christ, but He chose to keep them secrets, perhaps because the journeys of these men were not complete. These words described where they were at that moment— a snapshot in their lives—not who they would become through it all. God's mercy. A mercy He extended to them, until they rescinded theirs. A mercy He wants all people to emulate.

I think of that when people are different. I remember it when I stand alone in an action or a belief. I recite it, covering myself with it like a shield when the easily offended sharpen their verbal knives. Snapshot. Mercy. Human nature yet to be transformed.

It used to make me angry, but not so much anymore. My expectations are different. I've seen my own dark and, face-to-face with it, my pretensions smashed, I have no strength to carry stones.

Ends dangling. Lines undone and swinging, all catching us off-guard and

The days have been a feast of rich books and life-giving thoughts.

dragging us along life's path unceremoniously, showing our tears and cracks. I struggle to cover the ones I see in hopes that in the grand scale, it will cover my own. I try to repair the bridges. I hold up the bonds. I refuse to highlight the minutiae. I believe that mercy reigns, and tolerance is a medal that we get to wear on our breast after many long years of recognizing ourselves in the loose ends of others.

MARGARET
BECKER

In all its glory, it's about love—is it not? Both the gift of it and the receipt of it. It's about our belief in that love, our belief in the demonstration of that love, our honoring that love by extending it to others. I believe that is Jesus. I believe that for those who recognize it as such, it should be more than enough.

These

are my mother's hands

   that fly across the keys,

   the same square nails.

It is her spirit
within me

that

will

not go

quietly.

I've been raised

by a wild Irish poet.

I consider her bravery,

   and I make promises to

   continue the tradition. . .

AFTER
LABOR DAY

"**Y**ou know, you're not supposed to wear white after Labor Day," Debbie said, motioning to my pants.

"I've never heard that." I really hadn't.

Debbie seemed baffled by my response. How could any woman arrive in her twenties and not know? "Your mother never told you that?" she asked incredulously.

"Deb, you don't know my mother. She told me many things. That was not one of them. And frankly, with good reason. *Who made that rule?*"

Debbie didn't know, but follow it she did, because she didn't want to go against the grain and have people perhaps snicker behind her back. She was firmly rooted in the After Labor Day Sorority and its many edicts.

My mother never mentioned the sorority, nor, as far as I could see, did she pay homage in any way. She was nonconformist from the time she could make up her own mind. Not for the sake of being wild, as so many are, but for life's sake. She refused to don the velvet tether of meaningless expectation and follow along blindly. If the rules made sense, she adopted them as her own. If they existed solely to meet some artificial measure or standard, she just ignored them.

Mom wore white year-round, if it suited her, and bright lime, and pink, and Levi's 501's well into her seventies. She climbed mountains in her forties and delighted us all when, exhausted by the experience, she slid down the descent on her derriere. She went to college the same years I did, quickly becoming a campus favorite. She sipped coffee at the student union with partiers and intellectuals alike; they saw her ease with herself, and they became at ease around her.

Time and her placement within it were relative. Age was relative. She based validity on many things, none of which included the condition of her skin, the color of her hair, or the number of spots on her hands.

Don't get me wrong—she still had her beauty tools. Ruby red lipstick (a staple for any occasion that required leaving the house; the rest of the time, optional). High heels. And a few pair of clip-on earrings. But she controlled them. They did not dictate to her. For the most part, she went through life *au naturel,* with no apologies.

As the years met her, I never saw her shrink from their direct light. She wouldn't hide or curtail according to some cardboard image and her juxtaposition to it. I never

I've got nowhere to go. And days upon days to wreak havoc on the stoic internal scheduling that has been ingrained in me over the years.

MARGARET
B E C K E R

saw her question her standing on any level, physical or otherwise, although I'm sure she had her moments. She was peaceful in her journey, content in the mystery of it all. She lived within that belief and people recognized it, their respect for her mirroring her own.

As I got older, I realized that there was an order I was not privy to—an inverted value system where the outward becomes elevated over the inward and the temporal outweighs the lasting. I've watched women, significant women, pull back from life and live bordered existences because they felt they were less than they truly were, based on that system. Media influences culture all for the bottom line, ultimately. "Buy this and look better"—according to whom? "Wear that and look more like someone else. . . . Appear to be ten years younger than you are." *And why?* I ask myself. *What can possibly be the reason for such contortions, such blatant disregard for the universal process we call life?*

It's sad. It's disrespectful and perhaps worst of all, it's robbery, causing living beings to move and feel at half capacity, all for foolish and transparent reasons.

I consider my mother, garden dirt on the knees of her jeans, greeting neighbors at the grocery store. Fifty-five, in a red flannel shirt and hazard-light-orange mittens, and keeping vigil in the picket line outside of the nuclear plant, warming herself against the winter night by an oil-barrel fire. Her face crinkling into a pattern of laughter as she dances with my father in the kitchen.

Not afraid. Not affected. Happy for the days. Deep beauty, fresh and multilayered. Full of life.

I sit at my computer now in white pants. It's February. These are my mother's hands that fly across the keys, the same square nails. It is her spirit within me that will not go quietly. I've been raised by a wild Irish poet. I consider her bravery, and I make promises to continue the tradition. . . .

I will wear suede shoes in the summer, and long-flowing black capes when my hair is white and fractious. I will dance in sleeveless gowns until my legs refuse to cooperate. I will play games of hide-and-seek with children long into summer nights. I will squint into the sun, and strain to see the mist rising off the mountains, with no regard for their evidences on my face. I may even do "the bump" at my fiftieth high-school reunion, if my hips hold out.

This is the dowry of the Bohemians, the spoils of the spirited. I am rich beyond measure, imbued with their beauty as they trickle through my days.

The "schedule" voice is insistent and always starts its chiding with "I should. . ."

SEVENTEEN
AFTER LABOR DAY

In an attempt to break its iron grip, I am casually answering with a "Naah . . . don't really have to do anything." It goes against everything in me, but I've got to dig in my heels and relax.

"Hmm . . . Mawwgret,"

she says, smiling.

"Now I didn't know

why the Lord had me to

come here to get a job

in the collection department.

But I'm looking at you" —

"and I think I know.

You it, Mawwgret.

Oh, girl.

QUINTELLA
TURNS

**she
laughs
heartily—**

You know Him, don't you!"

The hair on the back of my neck prickles as she walks by my desk. I study her as she passes. She doesn't walk like other people, self-conscious and hurried. Quintella *sashays*.

"Mrs. Becker . . . Mrs. Becker?" my client's voice searches for me in the tiny ear bud. "Umm . . . yes, I'm here. Just one moment, please." I stand and look down at Mary over the half wall that separates our desks. We are both part of several parallel lines of women bound to chunky old wooden desks that are stained with ink and coffee. "Who's that?" I whisper, motioning to the new arrival.

In the middle of a call, Mary just shrugs. The fluorescent lights fill her glasses, so I can't see her eyes. I'm left to guess whether the indifference is true or feigned.

"Yes, Mrs. Santelli—I do need for you to make that payment very soon." I continue with business, sitting back down. "In fact, I need it before the first of next week. . . . Uh, ma'am, I. . . . Hey, now! There is no reason to revert to that kind of langu—Mrs. Santelli! Mrs.—"

I hate this job. I hate the pea-green carpet, the way they line us up like poster girls posed for some advertisement encouraging women to join the work force during World War II. The women in those ads, buxom and smiling, looked nothing like the women in this room. Nobody is smiling. Super-size Tums containers sit half-empty next to tiny pictures of family—all reminders and aids to keep us dreaming of the real world, the one we can't see from this windowless cavern.

Bill collections. There is no nice way to ask for money from people who are having a hard time feeding their children. A dollar might as well be one million dollars. They just don't have it. If they do, it goes for food.

Quintella settles in a few desks ahead of me. The mystery is unfolding. Another prisoner for the chain gang. But a bit of confusion ensues. I watch as our supervisor, Myra, comes over and gathers Quintella's supplies, pointing her to the desk directly in front of me.

I drop my head and begin dialing the next "S" client. This doesn't stop Quintella from engaging me. I hear her gently humming under her breath as she sits down with an unfettered southern sway. Once the pen and phone script are in place, she seems to pique for moment, like a retriever smelling scent. She scans the room. Some weird radar hones. Closer . . . closer . . . slowly she swivels in her chair until her eyes burn a hole in my scalp.

She knows I know that she's looking.
I notice fresh iron creases on the sleeve of
her neat, conservative dress, and hope I'm
wrong. Sensing my discomfort, she releases
me, picking up my nameplate.

"Hmm . . . Mawwgret," she says,
smiling. "Now I didn't know why the Lord
had me to come here to get a job in the
collection department. But I'm looking at
you"—she laughs heartily—"and I think I
know. You it, Mawwgret. Oh, girl. You know
Him, don't you!"

Before I have a chance to respond,
she adds, "But you haven't been so faithful
lately, have you, sister? No. I guess it's been
tough out here calling these poor people.
You don't like it, do you? But never mind.
I'm here now and we got some work to do."
Giggling the way people do when they know
something you don't, Quintella swings back
into place, righting her black vinyl purse
on the floor near the wall. She still hums.
I recognize the tune as a spiritual classic.

I begin cutting deals with God.

"Okay. You've had me here longer than I
thought I could take. I hate this place and
die a million deaths to think this is my fate.
And I know it's no secret that I haven't been
exactly . . . well . . . upstanding lately. But I

I am tired.
Fried.
Broken in a
million pieces.

am tired. Fried. Broken in a million pieces. I'll get it together, though. I'll turn the corner today. I just don't want to take this 'trolley of revelation' with this lady. I know what she's thinking and I know that You've got a lot of dirt on me. Please! This is my workplace. I don't want any trouble here. So here's the deal: I turn, You shut down the pipeline of info. We're square. Oh . . . in Your name, amen."

When I open my eyes I notice that Quintella is on a fresh wave of giggling. It's almost spooky.

The tutelage begins. My own personal revival series from eight to six, taking place all over that carpeted jail cell. From the bathroom to the weekly meetings at the microfiche machine—Quintella speaks. Quintella rebukes. Quintella heals. God moves.

The words I learn to love and hate: "Uh, Mawwgret, I'd like to have a word with you, sister." And then under her breath: "Been fasting for you, girl, all weekend long." Sometimes these encounters end graciously: "Now, look. I know what you did last weekend, honey, and I'm not going to embarrass you, girl, but you got to stop that." Like an aunt, sister, doctor—no condemnation, just concern with a dash of disappointment.

She walks in this bubble of anoint-
ing, under a higher authority, a more urgent
call than getting money from those "poor
people." Even her style of collecting bills
demonstrates it. Most calls, I can't hear her.
She cups her hand over the phone—doesn't
like those new ear buds at all. Think they
look too much like leashes.

Once I did hear her, though. "Yes,
Mr. Tantello. . . . I unnerstand, Mr. Tantello.
I been there, but let me tell you something.
I know a God who owns a thousand washers
on a thousand hills—and He can get you
one! But you got to serve Him, Mr. Tantello.
You got to give your heart to Him and He
will get you through this time."

I thought for sure her blatant talk of
God would get her sent to the door, hat in
hand. "Quintella! Quintella!" I was desperate
to get her attention. I wanted to stop her
before she went too far.

"Excuse me, Mr. Tantello." Turning
to me, covering the mouth piece, patient
with my interruption, she asked, "What is it,
Mawwgret?"

"Quintella, you can't talk like that
to these customers. It's against policy. You're
going to get fired!"

*Like a cat who
bends into a pet,
I take a deep
breath, arching
my back and
closing my eyes.
This place, these
sounds, they are
heaven to me.*

Rolling her brown, almond-shaped eyes to the ceiling, she tolerated me. "Mawwgret. It is better to *be* fired than to *burn* in the fire."

My jaw drops. I can't believe it. Although I don't agree with her methodology, I know she's moving in something I've yet to experience, and that she will be all right.

After five years, the day of emancipation finally arrives. Quintella is leading me out. Monday morning at 8:15, she sweeps by my desk, mock file in hand. "See me at the microfiche in ten." My first reaction is to trace my steps of the prior weekend. Where did I go? What did I do? I'm relieved when I realize it holds no turmoil.

At the microfiche we pretend to look up details on screen. I make myself nauseous with the moving images. "Good news. Mawwgret, I been praying for you this last weekend, and the Lord said something new. He told me you're gonna sing!"

"Gonna sing" came wrapped in that tone people use when they are completely convinced, beyond a shadow of a doubt, about what they are saying. It sounds like a big finish to a public introduction.

My hair is on end again—something I've become accustomed to. "Me?" I stammer. "Me? Sing—you're kidding. Really?"

"Yes, girl. Your time's about done here. Now me—that's another thing. I'm not released yet." Quintella says this wryly as she surveys all the other "needs" in the room. "Oh glory, girl! Good for you! But now listen. He told me that you have to start your ministry at my church."

I've never been to Quintella's church—physically, that is. I've sat in her church *here* every day for the last three years. I know what that church is like, and I have a sneaking suspicion about the other. I am dwarfed—on every level.

The next Sunday, I walk with my brand-new acoustic guitar through a burned-out part of New York and up the freshly painted steps of the compact white building. I've come a little earlier than planned. Thought I might warm up a bit—get used to the room in order to calm my nerves. It turns out I'm not early enough.

A few "sisters" have beat me there. They've come to warm up the place, too, but in a different way. I hear the choir of jubilation wafting out the door. *Heated belief flushes my ears.*

Distinctive, soulful voices ushering attitude. A little praise gathering, I suspect, but full of all of the fervor I've ever heard in any concert environment. "Thank You, Lord! You are worthy, Father! You are good. Umm-hmm! We know it's true, Jesus! You are sooooo good to us!" All in free-form eclectic scat, with only hands as accompaniment; both keeping time and applauding the especially vibrant moments.

At the top of the vocal heap I hear Quintella's singing voice cut through. Hoarse with many Sundays, imbued with the passionate angst I've watched her bridle day after working day. The choir has died down to murmurs and my hand is on the door when Quintella wails, "And don't scare Sister Becker away!"

I'm frozen in midstep. I am scared. Scared by her gifting, scared to believe. Scared not to. Scared to take my paltry offering in the door. There is more "ministry" in this unpretentious moment than I know I'll ever bring. *But I walk in anyway.*

The creak of the floor gets their attention, and once again Quintella turns and stops to take notice of me. Her hair is pulled back simply in a bun, her lovely brown skin is shining, her white-gloved hands are clasped in front of her dress. She inclines her head slightly to one side. "Mawwgret"—a greeting I suspect is reserved for a true sister or brother in this house. I feel her love for me, her pride in me, though she has carried me the entire journey. Her friends slowly study us both, and I wonder if they have the gift, too.

She invites me up to worship with them. When I take my place next to her, she assesses me from the side. The brim of her wide hat dips as she releases me with one long nod-and-blink combination. I am settled and stirred, and I know I am freed.

EIGHTEEN
QUINTELLA
TURNS

"To feel is to grow.

To grow is to live," I say,

concluding my thoughts.

My words make me

feel comfortably awkward

like a child in her mother's

OF
LEATHER

favorite high heels—

I am
much
too
small

for the true depth of these words,

yet I stand within them,

dreaming of the day

that I can walk

in their elegance.

This morning as I made my way to the coffee-maker through the grey shadows of the early day, the striking contrast of the orderly candles set against the wispy patterns of the roses caught my imagination.

"If only my heart were made of leather," she whispers as she turns her head away. Maddie chooses each word carefully. I see a single tear gathering at the edge of her eye, a shadow of the storm that lies beneath it. "I don't want to feel," she says. "It's a burden." She looks at me, her mouth set.

I know it's partially true and so I sit mute, shifting slightly in the car seat. The leather creaks under my leg, punctuating the silence. As I face Maddie more squarely, I think of how ill-prepared I am for this discussion. These are the answers I surely don't know. Time has brought me only more questions on the subject.

It's a Monday afternoon and we somehow have drifted from a simple coffee break to the deeper issues of life. It's around three o'clock and through the window's gray tint I watch schoolchildren streaming by us in twos and threes, their energy making me feel lethargic in comparison.

We stay like that for awhile, me studying her against the backdrop of the window of the car, her forming the next revelation as it unfolds.

"There's too much pain, too much discomfort that comes with the ability to feel," she says. A lone, fat tear slides down the side of her nose, fast, as if it's been held too long—the heat of the emotion that caused it already past. She wipes it away without drama. "Don't you ever not want to feel?"

I take in a lungful of air and blow it out with an ironic pump. "Yes," I begin warily. "Sometimes I wish my ability to feel was limited. Not too high. Not too low. Just in the middle.

"I imagine that there in the middle is some kind of agno-bliss . . . you know, where you don't know what you're missing, so you don't feel sad about it. And because you don't feel very deeply, you are somehow leveled to a light state of satisfaction, like in TV shows from the early sixties: everyone is happy just to go to work and to come home and change into his slippers. No one is feeling the wrenching struggles of life. No one is hurt beyond repair and no one is overcome with deep revelation."

I think about that and add, "No one is dynamic, either—but it does look comfortable, doesn't it?"

Maddie "harrumphs" in assent—I think—as we watch the last of the children turn the corner and disappear. We retreat into our separate worlds. I think about Mary Murphy, a coworker from a long time ago. Mary felt.

What beauty, these visions sitting here alone in the dark three nights now.

NINETEEN OF LEATHER

They all deserved their moment to speak, so I lit the duo and drank the sight in. What a magnificent combination. Roses by candlelight . . . shadows and folds, red wrappings deep and mysterious.

Mary: breast cancer twice, resulting in a double mastectomy. A daughter who took her own life. A son whose battle with drug dependence caused him to steal Mary's life savings. A husband who suffered a heart attack and couldn't work anymore, making Mary the sole supporter of her fragmented family.

My friend Mary, who at fifty-six years old was the most pummeled person I knew. She had been dealt more than her share of opportunities to feel. And she allowed it. She weathered it. She survived it and even wrestled with it until she squeezed the last bit of beauty and grace from each hideous blow. Mary, indelibly marked with lines both strong and delicate. Lines—tracks left by feeling, feeling it all.

She should have been bitter. She should have been angry, resentful—even finished with feeling anything. Yet it was Mary who noticed my difficult days at work. It was Mary who attempted to comfort me in my minor troubles. Empathically empowered, quick to take on everyone else's burdens as if they were her own—she seemed almost otherworldly at times.

Mary had let feelings touch the most vulnerable parts of her being without being destroyed by them. She learned the

perilous skill of allowing pain to transform
the essence of who she was, letting it break
her into tiny pieces, believing in the whole-
ness on the other side. Yes, Mary took it,
perhaps not willingly at first. But certainly,
somewhere along the way, she saw the pattern
of hardship amassing, like a hurricane gathering for the third time in a season, and understood she had no power to stand. No place
to run. It was then that the wisdom of the
broken surely came, and she knew to bend
in the process.

      One of the shattered people, Mary's
essence was recognizable right away. Calm,
steady, humble . . . loving. Slow to speak,
to anger. Nonjudgmental. Reverent. Not
because someone told her to be that way. Not
due to extreme discipline. But because she'd
been smashed to bits, and she felt every blow.

      Mary's breaking shifted the yolk
of her personality from one-dimensional,
edged flat glass into a beautiful prismatic
gem with millions of cracks and shatters.
Smooth on the outside yet crumbled within,
the very appearance seems itself a riddle:
how could something that looks so fragile
from a distance—ready to break at the
slightest vibration—be found, upon closer
inspection, to be so strong and serene?

"To feel is to grow. To grow is to live," I say, concluding my thoughts. My words make me feel comfortably awkward, like a child in her mother's favorite high heels—I am much too small for the true depth of these words, yet I stand within them, dreaming of the day that I can walk in their elegance.

"What if I don't want to grow?" Maddie responds, concealing a smile. It is my signal that the seriousness is over and silliness is coming.

"Can't help you there, pal."

We both know that we haven't really begun to feel—not to the level that we could. We're no Marys. Leather hearts seem not only unnecessary, but almost foolish. What little bad we have felt looks like a cakewalk. We have been granted the lesser demands of feeling and overall, I realize, it is a privilege.

"I *feel* like some ice cream," Maddie says as she starts the car.

"We know nothing," I say.

"True, so very true," she banters back, with a feigned wisdom meant to mock us both. We are so very young in so many ways.

SHINY
THINGS

It's never easy

to admit foolishness,

and yet admission

is sometimes

the only barrier

between

unrest and peace.

My marshmallow was almost dripping into the fire, completely crispy—just the way I like it. There on our yearly camping trip, my knees were two patches of dirt and fresh scrapes.

In a loose-tooth trance I sat, working one of my front stragglers back and forth, anxious for the big payoff: Tooth Fairy money—a whole dollar. My father noticed. "Stop doing that, Mag. It'll come out by itself. Leave it now." To get my mind off the task, he drew my attention elsewhere.

"Don't leave anything shiny lying around the campsite," he said casually, glancing up at the stars.

"Why?"

"Raccoons take it."

Raccoons! They take shiny stuff? No, they don't. Skeptical but hoping it was true, I asked, "Like what?"

Swirling the droop of his marshmallow back around the green branch he offered, "Oh . . . tin foil, dimes, jewelry. Anything that's shiny and catches their eye."

It didn't make sense. "Why?"

"Because shiny things get their attention. They can't resist."

Imagine that. Raccoons like shiny things. I had a new respect for the raiders that

I feel as if I am at a definite crossroads. It's frightening, yet freeing.

demolished our Coleman cooler every night, leaving only eggshells and crumbs behind. I liked shiny things, too. The quarter-sized sequined circles that were embroidered into the old ladies' hats at church. The mercury in the thermometer. New pennies. The chrome fender on my Stingray bike. The keys on the school janitor's belt. They were all eye-catching, glinting in the light.

I'm studying the stars tonight, from a different corner of the earth. They still wink at me from their velvet curtain and I half suspect that if I could, I would seize one of them and drag it back to my own "lair." The sound of the ocean's waves lapping the shore is a lullaby to me, and as I watch glittery sparks of moonlight dancing off its peaks, I'm reminded of my fascination with light and sheen. It has not abated now that I am an adult. The spoils are much larger now, though, because I've made the leap from object to emotion, driving the desire into deeper, darker recesses.

I've spent the entire day staring at this very same scene, writing intermittently. The privilege of creating, changing thoughts into words, is one I've dreamed of my whole life. Underneath this reflective sky I examine it here in my grasp. It's wrapped up in a silver

bow in its true light; a gift to me. Priceless.
I muse over that for a moment and trace the
steps that brought me here.

The desire to communicate. The desire
to encourage through that communication.
The passionate need to express. What a
wonderful inception these scribblings have
had. I write because I must. If I don't, I feel
like I'll explode. Yet there have been times
when my hand has glided over the blank
page, projecting me into the future. Not
the future of true response to those word
combinations, though, but to the cellophane
responses.

Praise? Dismissal? The tinsel chorus
of "wow and wonder". . . what will these
sentences bring? The question appears subtly,
at the base of my stomach, disguised in the
costume of responsible expression, clear
thought. But I've seen the truth unclothed,
wandering in my dark. It is the quest for
more and many. And though I've known
it for many years, I am still startled by the
sharpness of its angles, the unflattering pitch
of its growth. *The drive—all for something
suspect, at the expense of something pure.*

It's never easy to admit foolishness,
and yet admission is sometimes the only

barrier between unrest and peace. I've rooted around in my life for foil trophies far less valuable than the exquisite task of expression before me, far less meaningful than the discovery of these thoughts tonight.

A notion of "success" stirred my raccoon soul. The pursuit of it kept me motionless and dissatisfied, although I was a flurry of action. But I didn't understand the true meaning of the word, not in its brilliance, because if I had, I would have recognized success living and breathing right in front of me: in every minute stroke of the pen, every precious moment granted me for the sole purpose of creating, every job well done for the sake of inner satisfaction. I would have venerably gathered that true success up, esteeming the intent, the actual life of the moment. I would have seen the diamonds in the discovery of my creative voice, the rubies littering the road to the work's completion.

I would have passed the garland. I would have forgone the cellophane. I would have stared at the stars longer, complete in the task of scribing their silent revelations, beginning with that night of marshmallow wisdom.

It's been a long process of unraveling, yet I have come to recognize those "ringed eyes" in my own. As I pack up my blanket and candle tonight I'm remembering our family campsite; the tin foil strewn in pieces, marking a trail to the spot where I kept vigil as a girl, hoping to catch a glimpse of a marauder I felt I knew.

He never showed himself, but I knew he was there. He's with me now. He teases me with his nocturnal dances, his frequent wanderings to the frays for something to prick his dull eyes. I chase him, but he eludes me still.

I think of the word

community

　　and how antiquated

　　it seems

　　in this day and age,

yet I dust it off

and

commit

to care

　　for both those

　　bound to me

　　　　by blood

　　　　and those

　　　　bound

　　　　by proximity.

FIFTY
FEET

Little Lillian from next door stands at the base of my ladder. I'm 25 feet up, caulking the cracks in my wooden siding.

The question of the day is, "But why, Mar-grit?" In her language, my name is two syllables and she loops the second one up in the form of a question.

I don't like it up here, jerry-rigged with a cut-off bleach bottle full of spackle and a caulking gun in my tool belt. I know I'm an accident about to occur, but the last time I paid someone to do this I was out several thousand dollars and not satisfied. I'm a telephone repairman's daughter, for goodness' sake—I know I can do this. With a little help from my friends, that is—three to be exact. One held the ladder now, trying to distract Lillian.

"Lillian, what are you going to do today?"

"Umm . . ." she casts a glance up at me. "Pro'ly stay here. Mar-grit, why are you doing that?"

Oddly enough, I'm in the throes of asking myself the same question, but my mind is preoccupied with balance, sequence, making a good seam, and this hornet that seems intrigued with my shampoo. "Well, Lilly," I call down, "everybody has to paint their house

so that the water and snow won't seep in."
Kind of true. I think I'm getting vertigo.

"We don't paint our house."

Good one. "That's right, Lillian.
You don't paint your house because it's made
out of brick. It doesn't need to be painted."
Lucky stiff.

"Oh."

My friend Debi asks Lilly aggressively,
"You know my name? You know my name,
Lillian?"

She's startled, but brave. "No.
What is it?"

"Toe-mee-kwa. That's my name."

"Toc-mcc-kwa?"

It's working. My bead looks good.
The hornet is in the gutter and Lillian is
mesmerized.

"Tomekwa. . . . Is that really your
name?" Lilly asks, smiling. In the window's
reflection, I see her on one foot now, knee
turned in coyly.

"What do you think?" Debi asks
roughly.

Lilly sorts it out. I'm climbing down
for some more spackle and to even out the
odds a little.

"I think you're lying!" Lilly says
definitively.

191

"Noooo." Debi shakes her head back and forth vigorously without looking Lilly in the eye. With one hand on her hip and full conviction she adds, "I'm not lying. My name is Tomekwa."

Debi is even scaring me a bit. When I'm on solid ground I intervene. "You believe that, Lil?" I ask with a hint of skepticism in my voice.

She picks it up and seals it with an immediate "No!" followed by a giggle.

"Good. Neither do I." I'm giving Debi the eye and a hard nod of the head. *Be a little gentler*, I'm thinking. But there's no need. *Lillian is tough.*

"Hey, lady!" she calls to Debi, the way people do in the movies to waitresses. That gets to Debi because she doesn't want to be called "lady" this early in life. She gives me my own eye back, with a little indignation attached. I'm on my way back up the ladder now that I'm convinced that Lillian can handle herself.

Debi presses the obvious. "How old do you think I am, Lillian?" she asks as she puffs on a cigarette, a habit she claims she doesn't have. The ladder jiggles and I remind her, "Uh, Tomekwa—how about using both hands to hold me still?"

Be a little
gentler, I'm
thinking. But
there's no need.

"Oh. Sorry, Mag." Debi lifts herself from her seated position on the third rung and turns around to do the job right. "So Lillian . . . how old do you think I am?" she prods.

I chuckle. This is a dangerous question.

Lillian takes some time with this one. "Well, you're not a mom. . . . And my sister Bonnie is 17. . . ." She gives Debi the once-over. Mind made up, she announces, "You're 20 years old!" In other words, very old to a five-year-old, but not old enough to be a mom.

Debi is very satisfied. "That's right, Lillian. I'm 20 and Margaret's 18."

She buys it because I'm nobody's mom and I still roller-blade out on the cul-de-sac just like Bonnie.

Her voice chatters on about her cat, her friends from the block, her brother. I keep sealing the caulk with the back of a plastic spoon, picturing myself at Lilly's age. I was chattering, too, to my friend Mrs. Cohen— white-haired, wise, intellectual, and somehow "hip" as well. We had regular visits on her back stoop over slim Fudgesicles. She seemed genuinely glad for my company, often perching me on the brick wall so we could be eye to eye.

I flash back to the time I fought with Melissa Morrow after school. We grunted and grappled until I finally got her into a headlock. To my surprise she bit me, all up and down my side. I was frightened to tell my mom, but the bites were bleeding. I couldn't just ignore them because Melissa's mom was sure to show up—in the melee Melissa's orthopedic shoes got thrown over the school fence into a swamp. I was in a dilemma. Whom to talk to . . . whom to tell . . . Mrs. Cohen.

"Oh, honey!" scrunching her nose, lifting her black cat-eyed glasses up a quarter inch, she blurted, "those are bites! Margaret—tell me what happened."

I told her the whole sordid tale. She listened without judgment and then gave me some sound advice: tell your mom and get a tetanus shot. *I listened.*

Telling Mrs. Cohen somehow made it easier to tell my mom. I don't know why, exactly. Perhaps the very act of saying the words to an adult, and seeing her response, gave me courage. It wasn't the last thing I would tell her, and by no means the biggest. But I knew that I could trust her. I knew she would keep a confidence if I requested it.

The most that I could ever hope to be is malleable. Someone who actually listens and considers a point. Someone who does not see it as a loss to concede their wrongs.

TWENTY-ONE
FIFTY FEET

Someone who is not afraid to change. With change comes the ability to be strong; because when one recognizes their own fallibility, the threat of it is diminished—and the freedom of growth develops. To be wrong is to be free.

I'm coming down off the ladder now, listening to Lillian skillfully navigate Debi's ironic humor. I'm wondering who this little girl will grow up to be. What will she struggle with? What will give her pause at the front door of her own home? What secrets will she wrestle with solitarily, because they seem too bad or too big? I'm hoping that nothing will ever feel that overwhelming to Lilly, but if there is an instance, I hope that there will be someone, a neutral ear, a trustworthy friend, a Mrs. Cohen.

It's just Lillian and myself after awhile. We're drinking chocolate milk. She drains the last bit from her glass and wipes her mouth with the back of her hand. Elbow on the table, blonde banana curls pinned up in two tiny blue barrettes, she holds her head in her palm while studying me. Her father calls, but before she slides off the metal chair with a screech, she looks me in the eye. "What's her real name, Mar-grit?"

"Debi. But she likes to be called Tomekwa."

She runs fifty feet across my lawn. I'm thinking of how small a distance that truly is, wondering if our friendship will always reach that far. My thoughts and prayers trail after her. I think of the word *community* and how antiquated it seems in this day and age, yet I dust it off in my mind and commit to care for both those bound to me by blood and those bound by proximity.

She turns back to me just before she opens her front door, "See ya tomorrow, Mar-grit."

"See ya," I call back with a wave. And I look forward to it.

TWENTY-ONE
FIFTY FEET

The sun gently warming my face.

The green

carpeting my peripheral vision.

The fishing boats

in the distance.

IRISH
SEA

The essence of melody

that still has not left me.

In spirit,

     I am lifting my hand

     and prodding the moment…

     Gelatinous, vibrant;

     every sense is electrified

     with the weight of it.

A small voice I don't recognize

yet feel a kinship to whispers simply, "I'm alive."

I traveled long and hard that summer: Australia, the United Kingdom, Norway, Germany, South Africa, Africa . . . and Ireland.

I'd dreamed of Ireland my entire life. My grandmother left its shores at 13 and lovingly deposited the remnants of it in my mother. She in turn offered it to us. From discipline to imagination, she made it her duty to expose us to its spell. We had many Irish visitors over the course of my childhood, all enchanting us with stories of leprechauns and other fairyish characters. Somehow, even as a child, I was knit to the land, the people, the folklore. I knew that part of me dwelt there even though I'd never been.

When it appeared on my schedule for my overseas tour, I was ecstatic. The promoter had arranged for me to stay at a fine old Irish country house, just outside Belfast. My hostess: Jo Hogg from the Celtic band Iona. It couldn't have been more perfect.

The love affair with soil and soul was consummated the minute I stepped off the plane in Belfast. It began with the scent of music somewhere in my interior—the same feeling you get after hearing a moving piece. It echoes. It remains long after the last note is struck. It swirled there, though I'd heard nothing to prompt it. All my other senses opened—bent to it. Along with it, a wave of fear: I could not leave this place. I felt the blast of a breeze as an invisible door shut behind me. The greater part of me was home.

I was in a stream of dreaming from that moment on. The road to Jo's house was a long strand of different shades of green. The old men in fishermen's sweaters, the women making their way back from the market with the day's groceries—it was all just as I had imagined.

Jo's house was, in truth, an estate: white stone buildings with black roofs surrounded by farmland. I pulled up the stone driveway to be greeted by Mallory, the resident Border collie. Herding me effortlessly to the door, she instantly became a constant companion. Jo met me there in mucking boots, feed bucket in hand, the presence of an earthy day's blush on her face. She had already taken Mack, her lone horse, for his morning run.

The Irish. I think of where to begin and I find my language lacking. Deep and ironic; humor and sadness thriving happily together like twins joined at the soul. Beautiful with the raggedness of prolific poets. Privately emotional, without expectation or offense. *Unpretentious.*

Soon I was at Jo's farm table in the kitchen, with three different bakers' breads before me. I didn't ask, even said I wasn't hungry. But the good hostess, she put them out anyway, and ate herself just to set the tone. The breads, grainy and rich, reminded me of my mother.

I settled into a second-story room that looked over a river. No one expected me to do anything except explore and do whatever I pleased. Mallory woke me most mornings, jumping on my bed momentarily, pushing me down to the breakfast table.

We spent the days visiting, nibbling, and rowing a tiny boat to the other side of the river with Mallory heralding our arrival from the bow. I relaxed. On the opposite shore, we walked along a well-worn path with friends, considering the ironies of life. We exchanged thoughts, passionately and free-form, on many topics, from love to politics.

One morning Jo offered, "Thought I might take you on my favorite drive through the northern coast. Would you like that?"

A deceivingly simple offer. "Of course. Let's go!"

Into the Saab we went. Discreetly,

music rose from the car speakers. Riverdance. It was just taking hold of Europe then. Brilliant Celtic melodies twinkled around me from every corner of the car. Green fields sprawled vertically all around us. Shepherds in tweed hats signaled their herding dogs. The dogs were small cursors, encircling the sheep with invisible lines, stealthily running for miles to secure every last one. From this interior I was inside the trained lens of a cinematographer. My mind, the negative. All this to the click and the lilt of innocent wisdom, life played out on the Uilleann pipes.

At times the roads were so narrow and winding that we could go no more than a few miles an hour. At times the glens were so breathtaking that we'd pull over, open the doors, and stand in silence. Waves of light wakened me, pricking a part of my soul I didn't even know existed.

We stopped for soda water and candy. We stopped for lorries. We paused for sheep. We stared at history.

Jo brought me to cliffs of Murlough Bay. It was there the embryonic passion that had been moving in my chest came to full term.

"A short hike, Margaret. Would this be okay?"

We climb.

We sit.

We sip.

And I meld

into living.

I looked at my shoes: hip but not hike. Still, I could probably walk a short way. "Sure. Let's go."

"Short" means something different to the Irish. Jo left me in the dust, vigorously climbing up a path she'd traveled many times before. I was winded, rendered breathless by both the pace and the scene.

It was summer. There was still a chill in the air. To the right of me, about 1000 feet down, the waves of Murlough Bay bashed against craggy cliffs. To my left, green fields that were portioned off by the British years ago for a form of fiefdom. The borders marking them were longtime reminders of the feud that embroils this country even today. Green and black, in intense shadings: nuances of color and texture I'd never experienced before.

We walked for an hour, to the highest of the high, rocks set upon a grassy peak. My hostess asked, "Are you afraid of heights?"

"No. But my sister and I have overwhelming urges to hurl our bodies off of high places. No worries, though. No one will hold you responsible."

She hesitated. She didn't know my humor well enough to discern the truth. Fact

She stares at me again, the search full on her face.

"It's me . . . Peggy . . . Margaret! Don't you remember? We lived next door to each other for a whole year."

was, we hadn't spoken much since I arrived. I think I'd been in a trance. "It's all right, Jo. I'm just kidding."

We climb. We sit. We sip. And I meld into living. The hues, the violent wind tousling my hair. The sound of mythological waves pounding on ancient shores. The sun gently warming my face. The green carpeting my peripheral vision. The fishing boats in the distance. The essence of melody that still has not left me. In spirit, I am lifting my hand and prodding the moment. Gelatinous, vibrant; every sense is electrified with the weight of it. A small voice I don't recognize yet feel a kinship to whispers simply, *"I'm alive."*

And I feel alive. Maybe for the first time. As if someone has scraped away a film of smudges from my mind. Nothing feels familiar. Nothing is assumed. I am from a different planet and I am experiencing earth for the very first time. I am tasting human sense as a foreigner. I am considering it all through this infant being who is newly in residence.

I wonder what I have done with the past few decades. I wonder how many things I've held without feeling them at all, how many sunsets I've seen without seeing.

Flash. Recognition. Her mouth forms the first few letters of my name.

TWENTY-TWO
IRISH SEA

The offer of dinner and a lift to the hotel is suctioned back with them. She's made a terrible mistake. She says her good-byes. I hide my smile. Guess my financial condition wasn't the only thing keeping me out of their sorority.

I wonder when I stopped believing in magic: the things that escape logic, delighting the part of us all that still wants to be shown there are other worlds, other places, other ways that we are not privy to, or owners of.

I am watching a lifelong dream burst into life in Technicolor, right in front of me, and I am sending love notes to the God who made it so.

I turn to Jo. "I have no words."

She looks out. "Nor I."

"The joyful sound of happy beautiful children filling the African air was the most amazing singing I've ever heard."

I'll *never* forget my trip to a village in Ghana, West Africa, where I met children who had something to sing about.

They were healthy, well-fed and in school. Their parents were learning new skills to better provide for the family. Their village now had fresh water and improved agriculture, and you could sense the community's new hope for a better future.

What made all of this possible? What gave the children a reason to sing?

The World Vision child sponsorship program— made up of people like *you* and *me*.

For only $22 a month you will provide things like medical clinics, wells and schools, creating an environment in which a child can grow and flourish. And through the daily example and witness of World Vision staff your child will learn about the love of Christ.

WORLD | **VISION**

Call now to help change a Child's life!

Toll free: (888)511-6424

World Vision U.S.
P.O. Box 70050
Tacoma, WA 98481-0050